Michel Renouard

A Tour of
BRITTANY

Translated by Angela Moyon

ÉDITIONS OUEST-FRANCE
13, rue du Breil, Rennes

BY THE SAME AUTHOR
(selection of works)

NOVELS
Lumière sur Kerlivit, Desclée de Brouwer, 1964;
ed. Elor, 1988.
Le Chant des adieux, 1976; 2nd edition 1979 (out
of print).
Le Requin de Runavel (with Jean-François Bazin),
ed. Elor, 1990.

LITERARY CRITICISM
Robert Ruark (1915-1965),
journaliste et romancier :
l'échec d'une réussite, Ph.D thesis,
Paris IV, 1986.

SCIENTIFIC JOURNAL (Ed.)
Les Cahiers du Sahib, Presses Universitaires de
Rennes, since 1993.

MISCELLANEOUS
Châtellerault, Ouest-France, 1986.

WORKS ON BRITTANY
(all published by Editions Ouest-France)
Romanesque Art in Brittany,
1980. Also translated into German.
Brittany, 1984. Also translated into
German and Italian.
A New Guide to Brittany, 1984.
Wonderful Finistère, 1988. Also translated into
German.
Wonderful Morbihan, 1990. Also translated into
German.
Wonderful Ille-et-Vilaine, 1990. Also translated
into German.
Wonderful Saint-Malo and the Emerald Coast,
1991. Also translated into German.
Dictionnaire de Bretagne (with Nathalie Merrien
and Joëlle Méar), 1992.
A Guide to Brittany, 1993. Also translated into
German and Italian.
Bienvenue en Bretagne, 1993.
Saints guérisseurs de Bretagne (with Nathalie
Merrien), 1994.

Front cover:
The Wild Coast (Quiberon Peninsula).

Back cover:
St. Nicodaemus' Chapel in Ploeven (Finistère).

The Wild Coast (Morbihan).

For Jean-Paul Gauducheau

INTRODUCTION

A region is first and foremost a geographical area with its own features and its own landscape. Brittany is a wide peninsula stretching over a distance of some 168 miles and covering an area of 13,127 sq. miles. It is flanked by the sea (the English Channel or the Atlantic Ocean) to the north, west and south. Wherever you are in Brittany, the sea is never far away - there are only 62 to 93 miles between the north and south coasts in Armorica. This explains the mild, damp, maritime climate. The temperature is seldom very low but there can be strong winds here, and incessant rainfall.

The region has a population of 3,850,000 with a blend of Latin and Celtic backgrounds that give the people several unusual traits of character (the tenacity, not to say obstinacy, of the Bretons is legendary!) although they are gradually ten-ding to die out as a result of the daily diet of Franco-American television programmes. There are Bretons who still understand the language of their ancestors, and in the country districts of Upper Brittany, the Breton-Roman dialect, Gallo, remains alive and well. Yet, real though they are, the Celtic origins of the Breton people are now far in the past.

THE ARRIVAL OF THE BRETONS

There is no documentary evidence dating the arrival of the Bretons. Connections between Armorica and what we now know as Great Britain had always existed, even during the period of Roman occupation. In fact, it was the Romans who encouraged the very first Breton settle-

Brittany, land of fishermen.

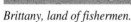

ments. However, it seems that immigration intensified during the 4th and 5th Centuries. Led by members of the royal families of Wales, Cornwall and Devon, Bretons apparently left their homeland to escape insecurity and pillage. Nevertheless, they were in no way a large invasion force, and it should be remembered that there were, at that time, only slightly more than 300,000 inhabitants in the whole of the Gallic Peninsula.

These seafaring Bretons settled mainly in the North-West. They ignored the East of the province and a part of the centre, if one is to believe the Gallo-Roman place names ending in '*ac*'. Moreover, according to François Falc'hun, the Armorican Celtic language still survives in the Breton spoken in the Vannes area, which would tend to prove that the Bretons did not overwhelm the already-existing populations and that the language of Rome did not entirely wipe out Celtic.

BRETONS FROM EVERY LAND...

Historically speaking, Brittany covers not only the region which today bears that name (the *départements* of Finistère, Morbihan, Côtes-d'Armor and Ille-et-Vilaine) but also Loire-Atlantique which is now part of the Lower Loire Region. It includes more than 1,500 towns and villages.

In addition to those who live within the peninsula, there are several million Bretons who have "emigrated" to France (especially the Loire Valley, Normandy, the Paris Basin and Dordogne) and to countries overseas such as North America, Argentina, the West Indies, Guyana, Australia, the Pacific Islands, and Réunion. This drain on human resources, which became most noticeable after 1850, has mainly affected Côtes d'Armor and Morbihan. One only has to travel to other parts of the globe to see the

Crozon (Finistère).

large numbers of diplomats, priests or teachers of Breton origin. However, wherever he may be, the Breton always remains attached to the land of his fathers.

THE BRETON LANGUAGE

The Breton language is more or less understood by 600,000 people, spoken occasionally by 250,000 (i.e. only 6.5% of the population) and read by 15,000 literary experts or militants. The decrease in the number of people using Breton as an everyday language, which was already noticeable after 1918, has risen spectacularly since 1950 (cf. the thesis written by Fañch Broudic, 1993).

Breton is a Celtic language like Welsh, Cornish, Erse, Gaelic, Manx (spoken on the Isle of Man) and, in days gone by, the language of the Gauls. In fact, it is closely linked to the first two of these languages forming, with Welsh and Cornish, the Brythonic branch. We should not, however, conclude from this that Welshmen and Bretons understand each other. Even though their languages come from the same source, the roots of the more common words are identical, and the grammatical structures are similar, there are more differences between them today than between, say, English and Dutch.

Breton draws much of its vocabulary from Celtic languages; indeed, some of it may be of Gallic origin. But from the late Middle Ages onwards, great use began to be made of words from Romance languages (French and the local dialects of Upper Brittany). Nevertheless, despite this overwhelming influence, Breton managed to maintain its grammatical individuality. Its verbal system in particular has remained rich and complex - as is its use of prepositions.

Glimpses of Brittany

Gorse.

Gorse: A shrub with thorny branches and yellow flowers (Papilionaceae family). Gorse grows on silicious soil and the Breton moors are its favourite haunt. It was grown until the end of the 18th Century as a fodder crop; it also provided bedding for cattle and brushwood for domestic fires. The commonest species is the European gorse which can be seen on dry moorland. Dwarf gorse prefers damper ground and Le Gall gorse grows on drier moors exposed to the wind.

Ankou: A personification of Death. Ankou appears in many different legends (cf. Anatole Le Braz' *La Légende de la mort chez les Bretons armoricains*) but always in the form of a skeleton dressed in a cape and carrying a scythe. There is also a maritime Ankou, the first person to drown in any one year. If Ankou appeared to the living, it meant that Death was imminent. Tradition has it that his kingdom lies within the Monts d'Arrée.

Celts: Peoples speaking Indo-European languages. They settled first in Central Europe before migrating westwards at the outset of the 2nd millenium. There is some controversy as to their background but certain experts believe that they came originally from Northern Europe. The Celts settled in what is now France and became the Gauls. They were the first Celts to invade Brittany. A second wave arrived with the Britons from across the sea in Britain who reached Armorica in or around the 5th Century A.D.

Passage grave in Commana (Finistère).

Death, known in Breton as "Ankou".

Dolmen: A megalithic monument. The word comes from the Breton *taol* (table) and *maen* (stone). The modern Breton word is *taol-vaen* (plural: *taolioù-maen*). It is, then, an impressive structure consisting of standing stones in the form of a table. In fact, the word "dolmen" applies to several very different structures. The oldest ones (6,500 B.C.) are round chambers. Others, dating from 5,000 - 4,000 B.C. are true dolmens. There are many of them in and around the Carnac area.

Parish closes: Religious buildings. Parish closes first appeared in the late 16th Century, gaining popularity and additional ornamentation in the 17th and 18th Centuries. A close normally includes a small wall enclosing the holy ground. The entrance is a gateway in the shape of a triumphal arch and some of them are extremely impressive. An ossuary (or funeral chapel) in the graveyard was used as a final resting-place for the bones of the deceased. A large calvary decorated with statues reminded believers of the Death and Resurrection of Christ. Finally, the main element in the close was the church, richly decorated with altar screens.

Saint-Thégonnec (Finistère).

Fest noz: A traditional form of festivity, like the Scottish ceilidh. The Breton word means "evening party". Originally, it applied to country people who gathered to celebrate the end of work in the fields. The parties included traditional dances and songs accompanied by music. People would drink cider. ***Festoù-noz*** are still popular in Brittany but have now lost all spontaneity.

Gwenn ha du, the Breton flag.

Gwenn ha du: The white (gwenn) and black (du) colours are those of the Breton flag as designed in 1923 by an architect named Morvan Marchal. The black stripes represent the bishoprics in Upper Brittany (Dol, Saint-Malo, Saint-Brieuc, Rennes and Nantes) and the white stripes the bishoprics in Lower Brittany (Léon, Cornouaille, Tréguier, and Vannetais). The ermines were the emblem of the Montfort family, once the Dukes of Brittany. Gwenn ha du was also the name of a secret society of Breton political activists founded in 1930.

Menhir: A megalithic monument. The word comes from the Breton ***maen*** (stone) and ***hir*** (long). The modern Breton word is ***maen-hir*** but the term ***peulvan*** or ***peulven*** (stone pillar or stone column) is also used (this is, in fact, the older word). Menhirs are found singly, laid out in a circle (cromlech) or erected in lines (alignments). The most famous standing stones in the world are in Carnac.

Océanopolis, the sea life centre.

Extract from ***Dictionnaire de Bretagne***
by Michel Renouard, Nathalie Merrien and
Joëlle Méar, pub. Editions Ouest-France, 1992.

Océanopolis: A Sea Life Centre opened in 1990 in the Moulin-Blanc yachting marina in Brest. With its 2,600 sq. m. of exhibition space and 500,000 litres of seawater in aquaria that are among the largest in Europe, the Centre gives visitors a chance to see some of the local flora and fauna of the Breton coastline i.e. fish, shellfish, seals, and algae. In 1992, a total of 400,000 people visited Océanopolis.

Saint Tujen (Finistère).

Pardon: Local religious festivals. The original purpose was a coming-together of congregations in order to seek pardon for their sins. The pardons were dedicated to the Virgin Mary, the Saints of the Church, then, gradually, to the Breton and Celtic saints. It is noticeable that pardons were often based on vows. In days gone by, pilgrims used to come on foot, sometimes travelling very long distances, in order to take part in a procession that lasted for several days.

The Megaliths

Carnac (Morbihan).

Mention Brittany and almost everybody thinks of megalithic monuments (dolmens and menhirs). This is quite understandable, for they are a very common sight in the region. The standing stones in Carnac alone number almost 3,000 and cover a distance of 2 1/2 miles. However, although the monuments were (eventually) given Breton names, they have no connection with the Celts, even if Celtic tribes were only too willing to use them as the background to their legends and dreams. In fact, the megaliths had already been in existence for 1,000-3,000 years before they arrived in the region. The stones are the remains of a period far back in time, the Prehistoric age when the peninsula was already inhabited by Man.

Anybody wishing to study this period in depth should go and see the quite remarkable collection in the *Musée de Bretagne* in Rennes (the exhibits are displayed in accordance with modern ideas on museum presentation) before going to visit prehistoric sites or other museums (e.g. Carnac or Vannes). One of the most representative of all the museums is the *Musée Préhistorique Finistérien* in Saint-Guénolé-Penmarc'h which is run by Rennes University.

A few rare, and discreet, remains of very ancient *Acheulian* tools (discovered in Cesson and, more particularly, in Damgan) prove that man was already present in Armorica c. 600,000 B.C.

During the very long period covering the *Palaeolithic* and *Mesolithic* Ages (500,000-4,500 B.C.), Prehistoric Breton Man left very few traces of his lifestyle. In this region there are no cave paintings such as those in Périgord (in any case, there are no caves), and no flint to make into knives. From the few discoveries that have been made, it would seem that the population was small in number. However, various artefacts from the Mousterian have come to light on Mont Dol (particularly scrapers). Right from the start, the population settled along the coast, a fact that underlined the importance of the sea.

In the *Neolithic*, or Late Stone Age (4,500-1,800 B.C.), a large population developed along the periphery of the peninsula. It left us the quite remarkable remains known as megaliths. This is not an isolated phenomenon. It is part of a general pattern; the *megalithic* civilisation stretched from the Iberian Peninsula up to Scandinavia.

Following the Ice Age, this was a period of increasingly warmer climates. It led, in Europe and the Middle East, to the introduction of an agrarian civilisation based on animal farming and crop production. This in turn brought about social changes and it seems to mark the beginning of the cult of the worship of the dead, as shown by the huge collective graves known as *dolmens* (this is the French version of *"taol-vaen"*, meaning "stone table").

During the 3rd millennium B.C., **menhirs** (literally "tall stones") were being erected. When they stand alone, they may perhaps mark a sacred spot but, although many hypotheses have been put forward over the years, nobody has ever succeeded in explaining their existence satisfactorily. Where the menhirs were erected in groups, they form a huge collection of stones either in circles (as at Larmor-Baden) or in lines (cf. Carnac and Erdeven), leading from East to West towards a semi-circular covered temple (Le Ménec in Carnac).

How were these menhirs and dolmens erected? Some of the stones weigh 100 tonnes and it is easy to imagine how difficult it must have been to roof over the graves using slabs of 15-20 tonnes. At La Roche-aux-Fées in

Saint-Just (Ille-et-Vilaine).

Essé, some of the 40-tonne slabs come from a spot 2 1/2 miles away. All of this presupposes a well-organised society in which the dolmens were perhaps the chieftain's graves (jewellery and jade axes have been discovered in some of them), a technically advanced society with its own architectural specialists. Moreover, these men produced and exported a type of polished stone axe which has been discovered in Great Britain, Holland and Alsace. In Brittany, the Neolithic Age site in Plussulien was worked for more than 1,000 years.

The peninsula passed from the Stone Age to the Age of Metal in and around the years 2,000 or 1,800 B.C, under the leadership of immigrants from across the sea. This was the **Bronze Age**.

The **barrows** were the work of an aristocracy of warriors and merchants which owed its supremacy to its

The megaliths were erected from 1,000 to 3,000 years before the arrival of the Celts.

Kerzhero, near Erdeven (Morbihan).

metal weaponry. There are more than 30 such burial places along the coasts of Brittany. They are individual graves built of dry stone beneath impressive mounds of earth 20-26 ft. high and some 160 ft. in diameter. Alongside the bodies are rich pieces of gold jewellery and de luxe weapons with gold-studded handles. A second, later group of barrows (1,450 B.C.) consists of approximately one hundred more modest burial mounds containing pieces of pottery in place of weapons.

The bronze-based economy developed rapidly. It made use of natural resources from the hinterland, such as wood and minerals, while becoming part of the Atlantic Coast trade route. Swords and heavy bronze or gold jewellery have been found. But there was a noticeable specialisation in the manufacture of bronze axes with straight heels (1,200-1,000 B.C.) which were exported throughout Northern Europe (Holland, Great Britain, Poland).

By 700 B.C. the Atlantic seaboard Bronze Age civilisation, which was then at its height, was producing shaft axes while the Iron Age was beginning to develop in the rest of Europe. This new type of civilisation expanded, and was soon to bring about the downfall of its predecessor.

From 500 B.C. onwards, ***Celtic*** people with their own languages and civilisations began to settle in Armorica, bringing with them the Hallstatt traditions (from the name of an Austrian village). It is difficult to assess their exact number but they do not appear to have totally supplanted already existing civilisations. At this same point in time, commerce was beginning to introduce Mediterranean influences (Greek and Italian) to the region. Once amalgamated and assimilated, these later movements gave rise to a regional ***Iron Age*** civilisation dating from the La Tène Period (so-called after an archaeological site in Switzerland).

The population settled in fortified ***oppida*** — coastal spurs of rock (Erquy) or hills (the vitrified forts in Plédran) — or in strongly defended camps (cf. the Artus Camp in Huelgoat). Graves no longer had the same importance as in the New Stone and Bronze Ages. Engraved tablets were erected, vaguely reminiscent of menhirs except for their regular shape tapering upwards from the base to the top.

The bronze industry collapsed, and very few iron objects have been unearthed. However, rich pottery (the

Carnac (Morbihan).

first of its kind in Gaul) was produced. The pottery had various colours, ranging from grey to red, and its form was similar to the metal recipients of earlier years. The decoration, composed of friezes and painted bands of colour with swirls and palm leaves, is of classical inspiration (Greek and Italian).

Celtic Armorica was divided into five independent "nations" (the tribes being the Namneti, the Veneti, the Osmismens, the Curiosolites and the Redoni). Their boundaries are still unclear today.

At the end of the 2nd Century B.C., when the Arverni people had lost much of their power, the "nations" minted gold coins similar to the gold stater of the Greeks. This was the case in the rich maritime Veneti "nation".

CARNAC, A MAJOR CENTRE OF PREHISTORY

Carnac (Morbihan) is one of the world's most outstanding prehistoric sites. The alignments in Carnac itself and in the neighbouring towns of Plouharnel and Erdeven now comprise some 4,000 menhirs but many have disappeared over the centuries.

Carnac.

On the Place de la Chapelle, the **James-Miln-Le Rouzic Museum** houses a collection of megalithic artefacts (polished stone axes, necklaces, and jewellery).

The mystery surrounding the standing stones in Carnac has never been satisfactorily explained. Some say that they were used for astronomical calculations; others believe them to have religious significance.

The standing stones are believed to date from the second half of the Neolithic Era (2,800-2,300 B.C.) They stretch over a distance of more than 2 miles from the hamlet of Ménec to tiny Kerlescan.

A GREAT MENHIR NEAR RENNES

The **porticoed dolmen** at la Roche-aux-Fées in Essé (Ille-et-Vilaine) is one of the largest megalithic monuments in France. It is of the "angevine" type, very rare in Brittany but quite common in the Saumur area. It was built c.2,500 B.C. The dolmen is 63 ft. long and the heaviest stone weighs 45 tonnes.

La Roche-aux Fées.

The Romans in Brittany

The Romans came by sea...

Continuing their triumphant march, Julius Caesar's armies reached Armorica in 57 B.C. The Veneti, allied to the other tribes, refused to submit to the invaders. Caesar had to have ships built so that he could attack from the sea in 56 B.C. It was a disastrous battle for the heavy ships of the Veneti; they were becalmed. Caesar's victory led to the disappearance of the Veneti's trade, and as it also cut trade routes to the British Isles, it marked the end of the maritime supremacy of Western Gaul.

From then on, Armorica was part of the Roman world. Latinisation was undertaken gradually within the ancient tribal boundaries. During the first two centuries A.D, towns were built - Nantes (Condevincum), Rennes (Condate), Vannes (Darioritum), Carhaix (Vorgium) and Corseul. Each had its own temples, theatres, gateways, luxurious houses, sewage system and water supply (the one in Carhaix is still visible). They had organised municipal hierarchies. Roman masonry techniques and the use of tiles became increasingly commonplace, even in country districts where luxurious *villas* were built, decorated with friezes and marble, and each with its own bath. A well-structured network of roads linked the towns to each other and to the rest of Gaul; it was not replaced until the 18th Century and some of the original milestones have survived to the present day (Berrien, Kernilis, Mespaul etc.).

Economic activity was based mainly on farming. The fishing industry supplied the raw materials to the curing and salting plants in the harbours. The goods made indispensable by the Roman way of life (ceramics, marble, amphorae of oil or wine) were all imported. Armorica's mines were also worked in Gallo-Roman times, producing silver, tin, lead and zinc.

CORSEUL, A ROMAN TOWN...

The territory of the Curiosolites, and its capital Corseul near Dinan (Côtes d'Armor), entered the history books in 57 B.C. Indeed, Julius Caesar mentioned it in his *Gallic Wars*. Little is known about this Gallic tribe except for the fact that it minted its own coinage, owned Jersey and traded with Southern Britain. From approximately 40 B.C. onwards, Corseul became a Roman *township*, possibly (but there is some uncertainty about it) called Fanum Martis before taking the name of Civitas Coriosolitum.

For 400 years, the town was a major Gallo-Roman settlement. Five Roman roads led to the town and Corseul traded with part of the Roman Empire stretching from Aquitaine to Toscany. It was especially prosperous during the latter part of the 1st Century A.D.

Corseul began to fall into decline in the early years of the 4th Century and soon Aleth (near what we now know as Saint-Malo) supplanted the former capital of the Curiosolites. The barbarians dealt the town a death blow: it was apparently burnt down c. 406 A.D.

There are few outstanding reminders of this era. Over the centuries, the Roman remains were pillaged. A few fragments (including a column topped by a capital) have been brought together in the gardens round the town hall. There are some more (bases of columns) in the Garden of Antiquities in the rue Lessard. Nearby, there is an **Archaeological Museum**.

The church (1838) contains a **Gallo-Roman tombstone** (1st Century A.D.).

Some 200 yds. from the church on the Saint-Jacut road is the **Champ-Mulon** archaeological dig. But the only spectacular monument is about 2 miles East of the town hall on the Dinan road, in the village of Haut-Bécherel. It is a *cella*, known as the **Temple of Mars**. The polygonal tower, which was probably built in the latter part of the 1st Century A.D. is evidence of the high quality and solidity of Roman buildings.

A NEW SITE: CHATILLON

A **Gallo-Roman site** (2nd and 3rd Centuries) was discovered in Noyal-Châtillon (Ille-et-Vilaine) in 1983, which is hardly surprising since a major Roman road passed through this spot. A large-scale archaeological dig was undertaken on the site between 1984 and 1987.

The Temple of Mars in Corseul.

Carolingian and Romanesque Architecture

St. Saviour's Basilica in Dinan.

Little remains of the Carolingian period — just a few coins, a few inscriptions on memorials, and a few manuscripts. There is, though, one outstanding gem — the Carolingian church in Saint-Philbert-de-Grand-Lieu (Loire-Atlantique). It is thought that the chapels in Pléchâtel (Ille-et-Vilaine) and Guer (Morbihan) might also date back to the early 10th Century. These, though, are the exceptions, even if it is commonly acknowledged that there were once many buildings from this period, all of which have disappeared over the years. Most of what has survived has been restored, extended, or even totally disfigured. Philistines among the clergy even went so far as to demolish Romanesque churches to make way for masterpieces - of consummate ugliness.

The feature that most strikes visitors is the robust, austere appearance of the Romanesque chapels and churches, which always look as though they are keeping themselves very much to themselves. The building materials (schist, granite and sandstone) add to their severity. The decorative features come from various sources (Ancient Greece and Rome, Nordic countries, the Orient, Moslem countries, and Ireland). The most common form of decoration is geometric, consisting of chevrons, cable moulding, intertwines, billets, circles, festoons, checkerboard patterns, and, most common of all, crockets).

Brittany has only one example of vernacular architecture dating from this period - the Plaids House in Dol. A number of castles were built in the 12th Century but, at best, they have survived only in the form of ruins.

A FEW TRACES OF THE CAROLINGIAN AND PRE-ROMANESQUE PERIODS

THE CHURCH IN SAINT-PHILBERT-DE-GRAND-LIEU (Loire-Atlantique)

Saint-Philbert is a small village to the South of the huge Grand-Lieu Lake. Its splendid Carolingian church has remained practically intact to this day, and is one of the few buildings from the period to have survived in France, or, indeed, in Europe.

The **church** lies in the centre of the village on a small shady square. Do not be put off by the exterior, which is unwelcoming at first sight and which hardly even stands out from the buildings on either side of it. It was deconsecrated in 1870 and had to be partially restored at the end

Saint-Philbert-de-Grand-Lieu.

of the 19th Century. It was the uppermost section that suffered most at this time; the present roof is almost 10 ft. lower than the original. Most of the church dates from the Carolingian period (9th Century). The transept was built in 819 A.D. The Vikings set fire to the church in 847 A.D. and the nave was not rebuilt until the 11th Century but with the same alternating stone and brick bonding.

The whole of the Eastern section of the church was rebuilt with a view to showing Saint Philbert's tomb off to its best advantage and ensuring that pilgrims could walk round it easily. It is one of the few examples (and one of the oldest) of an **upper crypt** with an ambulatory. The **nave** is the most important part of the building; a double row of mighty pillars support stone capitals.

To get the best view of the chevet, go round the left-hand side of the church until you reach the river, then climb the path beside the bridge. Nearby is the Lakeside Centre *(Maison du Lac)* which houses a small museum of birds and wildlife.

ST. STEPHEN'S CHAPEL IN GUER (Morbihan)

St. **Stephen's Chapel** *(chapelle Saint-Etienne)* in Guer (follow the signs to Malestroit then turn right onto the V7) consists of a simple rectangular chamber. Note the brickwork decorating the upper edge of the East gable. This is one of the oldest chapels in Brittany, thought to date from the end of the Carolingian era (10th Century).

MAJOR EXAMPLES OF ROMANESQUE ARCHITECTURE IN BRITTANY

DAOULAS (Finistère)

Building work began on the **church** (once a minster) in 1167 over the remains of a much older abbey. The church was altered on several occasions and underwent major restoration, in the Romanesque style, in 1877 when some of its monuments were displaced and resited elsewhere. The main parts of the building dating from the 12th Century are the West Front, the North aisle and the seven-arched nave.

The **cloisters** (c.1170) were rebuilt and completed during the 19th-century restoration (which means that some sections are, in fact, reproductions). It is an exceptional example of Romanesque architecture as it was in

St. Stephen's Chapel in Guer.

Brittany at that time (second half of the 12th Century) with its colonnettes and magnificent kersantite capitals. In the centre, an **octagonal lavatorium** is richly decorated with geometric patterns; it seems to be of Norman inspiration. At the East end of the cloisters is the wall of the **chapter house** with its two Romanesque windows.

LANLEFF (Côtes-d'Armor)

Ruins are all that are left of the circular pink granite "temple" of Lanleff, but they are interesting for more than one reason. The "temple" as seen today has a central rotunda with twelve semi-circular arcades, a circular

side-aisle with slit-windows and an apsidal chapel typical of the Romanesque period with a barrel vault.

The church was built in the late 11th Century (i.e. at the time of the Crusades) and was based on the design of the Church of the Holy Sepulchre in Jerusalem.

LANMEUR (FINISTERE)

The village lies on the site of the former Kerfeunten (literally, town of the fountain) which was razed to the ground by the Vikings in the 9th Century. There are still some traces of the old town left e.g. a Romanesque or pre-Romanesque **crypt** below the present church, which is

Opposite: The cloisters in Daoulas.

The "Temple" in Lanleff.

modern apart from the 18th-century tower (the church dates from 1904). The crypt is the only one of its kind in Brittany.

LOCTUDY (Finistère)

This seaside resort has the best-preserved **Romanesque church** in Brittany. Visitors should not be put off by the outside of the church and its tower, both of which date from 1760. The barrel-vaulted chancel, the groined arches in the ambulatory and the apsidal chapels are all splendid pieces of architecture. The nave, lit by a clerestory, has cruciform pillars. The capitals are decorated not only with crossettes, palmettes and spirals but also with crosses, animals, and human figures. They are a reinterpretation in granite of traditional Corinthian capitals. On several of the bases are quite distinct carvings of naked men and women.

The style of the early 12th-century building, which underwent restoration between 1845 and 1888, was influenced by its mother church, the Benedictine abbey in Saint-Gildas-de-Rhuys and, therefore, by the architecture of the Loire Valley.

MERLEVENEZ (Morbihan)

Like several other villages in the "Lorient Pocket", Merlevenez suffered severe damage during the last war. But a Romanesque **church** survived and was restored between 1946 and 1960. Its doorways are Romanesque. The 14th-century tower had to be rebuilt. Inside, the arches in the nave have subtly-decorated capitals. The roof of the transept crossing is set on a beautiful cupola supported by squinches dating from the late Romanesque period.

PLOERDUT (Morbihan)

Visitors should not be put off by the nondescript appearance of the outside of the church, parts of which date from every period between the 13th and 19th Centuries. Inside is a **Romanesque nave** with eight spans and cushion capitals decorated with geometric motifs (swirls, checkering, curves and broken lines). The sanctuary also has an ossuary.

Top: Merlenevez.
Middle and Bottom: The church in Ploërdut.

QUIMPERLÉ (Finistère)

Holyrood Church *(église Sainte-Croix)*, the former minster, is a gem of Romanesque architecture. It was built in 1083 but had to be rebuilt in the 19th Century when the central tower collapsed, almost totally destroying the church. Restoration work (1864-1868) was carried out with the utmost care and attention and the church was recreated as it had been before. It is built to a circular layout similar to the Church of the Holy Sepulchre in Jerusalem. It has a rotunda onto which open a porch and three apsidal chapels. The apse has withstood the test of time and is probably the finest of its kind in Brittany, with its windows, arcatures, pillars and capitals. The 11th-century crypt is still intact; its capitals, decorated like the ones in the chancel, are quite remarkable.

REDON (Ille-et-Vilaine)

St. Saviour's Church was once part of the abbey. Its **central belfry** dates from the 12th Century. There are three storeys of arcatures and the corners are rounded off. This is the only Romanesque tower of this size in Brittany and probably the only belltower in France with rounded corners. Outside, the apse is flanked by a fortified chapel (15th Century). The 14th-century Gothic tower, which has been set apart from the rest of the church since a fire in the 18th Century, gives some idea of the size of the nave in this the biggest Romanesque building anywhere in Brittany. The interior also shows how the church has been altered through the centuries. The long nave, transept crossing and some of the frescoes are Romanesque; the **chancel** dates from the 13th Century (note the superb triforium). Beneath the belfry, a cupola on squinches (something of a rarity in Brittany) covers the transept crossing.

One of the best places from which to admire the Romanesque tower of St. Saviour's is in the cloisters of **St. Saviour's College**.

SAINT-GILDAS-DE-RHUYS (Morbihan)

In the 10th Century, the first monastery was pillaged by Viking pirates. In the following century, at the request of Duke Geoffroi I, the abbey was rebuilt by a monk called Félix who was brought here from his hermitage on

Top to Bottom:
Holyrood Church (église de la Sainte-Croix) in Quimperlé.
The crypt in Sainte-Croix.
The belfry in Redon.

Saint-Gildas-de-Rhuys.

Saint-Gildas-des-Bois.

Ushant. The famous 12th-century monk, Abélard, spent ten or more years here.

The **church**, which the Benedictines altered in the 17th Century, has features dating from the 11th and 12th Centuries i.e. the chancel, transept, capitals and tombs. Some of the Romanesque capitals have been turned into stoups. In the sacristy is a remarkable treasure.

SAINT-GILDAS-DES-BOIS (Loire-Atlantique)

This small town, which once lay on the Roman road from Vannes to Blain, was called Lampridic when, in the early years of the 11th Century, the Lord of La Roche-Bernard decided to found a Benedictine abbey here. The present parish church is the former **minster**. It is a fine building dating from the 12th and mainly 13th Centuries. The North arm of the transept and the walls in the chancel and nave are 12th Century; the remainder of the church seems to date from the intermediate period between Romanesque and Gothic. However, it underwent considerable alteration over the years, especially during the 19th Century. It was bombed in 1944 and restored c. 1950.

From Gothic
to Renaissance

The cloisters in Tréguier (Côtes-d'Armor).

The **Gothic style** appeared at the end of the 12th Century, imported from the Loire Valley (cf. the vaulting in Saint-Malo) and more especially from Normandy and England. Cathedrals, abbeys, and more modest chapels were erected, and some of their features were to be commonplace in Breton architecture for many years, e.g. the large chancel ending in a flat chevet surrounded by the thick walls into which were cut deep embrasures (cf. Pointe Saint-Mathieu, Saint-Malo), geometric partitioning by means of heavy mouldings, the pillars, the surface of the walls, and the massive towers on either side of a vast porch (cf. Dol, Saint-Herbot, Saint-Pol-de-Léon, Pont-Croix). Note the very rare early 13th-century frescoes illustrating the legend of St. Julien in Le Loroux-Bottereau (Loire-Atlantique).

In the 15th and 16th Centuries, the **Flamboyant Gothic** style developed in the chapels that can be seen in their hundreds dotted across the countryside. They ensure that certain localities (e.g. springs or hilltops which are objects of popular worship) retain their sacred character.

One should not, however, be misled into thinking that they were the creation of the peasantry. Examples of a principality's style of architecture they may be, but they were erected either by Dukes anxious to gain publicity as indicated by the coats-of-arms sculpted on the front (cf. Le Folgoët, Locronan), by great families for much the same reason, or by rich merchants from the centres of maritime trade (Penmarc'h, Morlaix, Locronan). They were built by specialist teams of craftsmen who travelled the length and breadth of Brittany. This explains the common features that are typical of this art form, and also its great variety.

The most perfect of all these buildings are undoubtedly to be seen in Le Folgoët and Kernascléden. Occasionally the churches are connected to a small chapel; they are closed at the East end by a flat chevet containing a large window or, in the late 15th Century, by one of the three-gabled chevets that were developed and made increasingly popular by a group of craftsmen from Morlaix. The austere nave is almost always topped

The chapel in Saint-Herbot (Finistère).

A close-up of the figures on and around the Crosses.

A picture in stone.

Penmarc'h (Finistère).

by a timber roof with carved beams and corbels. It is separated from the single side-aisle on the South side by great ogival arches whose ribs delicately merge into pillars devoid of capitals. The wall running along the side-aisle is studded with wide windows. They ensure sufficient light and, on the outside, give the wall its characteristic granite saw-tooth appearance that stands out sharply against the great slate roof. A large porch, its interior decorated with statues of the Apostles, stands on the South side of the church. The commonest type of chapel is a low building encased in its roof and pierced with squat openings.

However, there are a good many tall churches with slender pillars creating a sense of space, especially in the towns and in the East of the region (Saint-Jean-du-Doigt, Grâces-Guingamp, Ploërmel, Vitré, Penmarc'h). The belfry is either a traditional Norman-style tower (often topped by an open-work spire surrounded by pinnacles and a balustrade as in Saint-Pol-de-Léon) or a more modest affair built on the gable end, lightly supporting the balustrade and pinnacles and flanked by a staircase turret. The church usually has an ossuary and a calvary, and sometimes a well (cf. Saint-Nicodème), all of which make up the parish close. Thanks to the use of kersantite

(a very fine-grained basaltic rock), the sculptures and carvings are both complex and elegant (cf. statues and carved foliage in Le Folgoët and Kernascléden). In some churches, pulpitum and rood-screens still separate the nave from the chancel (Saint-Fiacre du Faouët, Belle-Isle-en-Terre, Loc-Envel, Kerfons).

The Flamboyant Gothic style, which was totally integrated in Brittany and reinterpreted through regional traditions, remained for many years the most common means of expressing architectural creativity. No doubt it answered the population's need for permanence in their most deeply-rooted religious aspirations, but it also reflected social and economic structures, a mental attitude and the region's culture. The designs which were first perfected in the 15th Century continued to be copied right up until the 18th Century in country districts. Once tapped by deeper and deeper levels of society, they became symbols of a veritable popular art form.

The ***Renaissance*** appeared in the early 16th Century, while Flamboyant Gothic architecture was still at the height of fashion. Guingamp and Landivisiau, for example, were still being ornamented with pilasters and candelabra from the castles of the Loire Valley while altar screens, statues (the Immaculate Conception), stained glass windows (La Martyre, Moncontour) were imported from Germany and Italy, and the first copies made (cf. Champeaux, Dol). But from the end of the 16th Century and on through the 17th, the classic Renaissance style was widely adopted, becoming especially common in the Léon region. The bourgeois merchants, replacing the high-ranking and thenceforth resolutely Frenchified aristocracy, began to erect *parish closes*.

Church architecture remained unchanged. But it was decorated with a new type of ornamentation from Paris. The same was true of the porch, the great calvary, the triumphal gateway (cf. Berven, Saint-Thégonnec) and the ossuary, all of which were huddled magnificently together in the close. Craftsmen recreated in granite the Classical pediments, ringed columns and sheathed caryatids (cf. La Martyre) that they had seen in the architectural treatises of Philibert Delorme who built the Tuileries, or Jacques Androuet du Cerceau (1566). The great tower was topped by a dome or lantern (Pleyben) as was the fragile bell-tower on the gable end (cf. Roscoff, Sainte-Marie-du-Ménez-Hom).

The vestries embellished the interiors of churches with magnificent furnishings (in the 17th and 18th Centuries). Influenced by the Jesuit missions and preaching, by the Classical buildings in towns, and by the Lavallois altar screens (cf. Sizun), a great Mannerist or Baroque style of decoration that was both abundant and colourful, overwhelmed chancel and side chapels alike. Some are extraordinarily rich (cf. Commana, Bodilis,

Saint-Ségal, Brasparts). Statues of saints in Baroque costume, some of which were imported by the missions (St. Anne, the Holy Family) and Italianate Madonnas adorn niches and reredos. Richly decorated rood beams replaced the rood-screens which were dismantled as a result of a liturgical reform.

THE MOST FAMOUS PARISH CLOSES IN FINISTERE

COMMANA

The heavy gateway to the graveyard is decorated with lantern turrets, like the sacristy (1701) in the South-East corner. The ossuary-chapel dates from 1686. The **church** (16th-17th Century) has a square belltower with a stone spire (1592). The South porch (c.1650) is a fine example of Breton Renaissance architecture. The church houses the St. Anne **Reredos** (1682) showing the saint with the Virgin Mary and Jesus. Baroque enthusiasts consider it to be one of the finest altar screens in the Léon region. To the right are the Rosary Reredos and the Reredos of the Five Wounds. Also worthy of note are a number of statues including a wooden Ecce Homo, and the canopy above the font borne by five women representing the Christian virtues.

GUIMILIAU (Finistère)

A **triumphal gateway** leads into the close and on the right stands the highly ornate great **calvary**

Guimiliau: Eve being created out of Adam's rib.

Guimiliau.

(late 16th Century) including more than 200 statues. It retells several episodes from the Life of Jesus (not in any set chronological order) and the statues are dressed in 16th-century costume as was usual at that time.

The **ossuary**, dating from the mid 17th Century, includes an outside pulpit which was used for open-air sermons, especially on All Souls' Day.

The South **porch** (1606) on the way into the church is typical of the Renaissance style as developed in the Léon Region.

The **church** is a typical example of Breton Flamboyant Gothic architecture, embellished with a few Renaissance features, but it contains some remarkable late 17th-century furniture corresponding to the spread of the Catholic Counter-Reformation. The baptistry (1675) on the left is a masterpiece of Baroque craftsmanship.

LAMPAUL-GUIMILIAU (Finistère)

The graveyard occupies the centre of the parish close. It has a semi-circular gateway topped by three crosses (1668). Beside it is the **ossuary-chapel** (1667). In the middle of the close stands a very plain **calvary** (16th Century).

The West Front of the **church**, built in the Gothic style with some Renaissance decoration, is flanked by a belfry (1573) whose spire was struck by a thunderbolt in 1809. The nave and South aisle, in which the window bays are decorated with monsters and other imaginary beasts, both date from the first half of the 16th Century and are Flamboyant Gothic in style (except for the piers). The **South porch** (1533) contains the traditional statues of the twelve Apostles.

There are three real gems of craftsmanship inside the church. First of all, there is the 16th-century **rood-beam which**, of course, bears the Cross and statues of the **Virgin Mary and St. John. The St.John the Baptist Reredos** depicts, among other things, the life of the saint and certain episodes in the Life of Christ. The bas-reliefs on the side show the fall of the angels. The **Passion Altar Reredos** has eight sections and some of the statues are strikingly realistic. The two side panels are quite remarkable.

In the side aisle on the right is a canopied font (1651). The left-hand aisle contains a **Pietà** (1530) with six figures, all of them carved out of a single block of wood. Nearby is the impressive **Burial of Christ** (1676), one of the finest anywhere in Brittany. It was carved by a sculptor from the dockyard in Brest, a man who originally came from Auvergne.

LA MARTYRE (Finistère)

At the entrance to the close, above the **triumphal arch** (15th Century), is a platform and a 16th-century calvary. Carvings on the very fragile **porch** (c.1450) illustrate the Life of Christ and give some insight into contemporary society. There is also a realistic sculpture of the benefactor. On the tympanum is a later carving representing the Virgin Mary in bed. The shafts and arches of the porch are covered with cherubs and human figures. The porch also contains a stoup decorated with a figure of Ankou, or Death (1601). The **ossuary** dates from 1619. It was built of fine kersantite.

On the outside wall is a sheathed **caryatid** taken straight out of French Renaissance books on architecture.

The Laying in the Tomb, in Lampaul-Guimiliau.

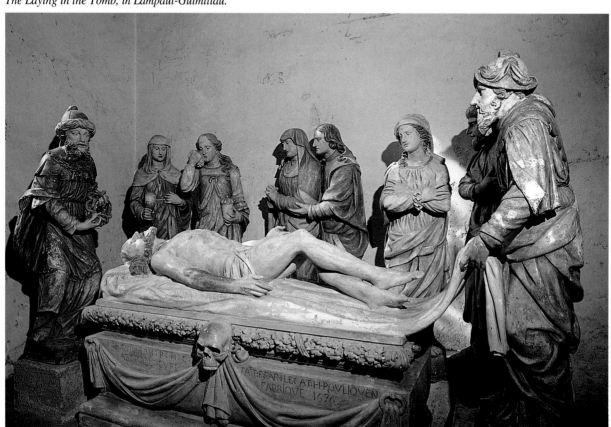

The most striking feature inside the **church** is the total lack of stylistic cohesion.

PLEYBEN (Finistère)

The **church** (1564 but with late 19th-century restoration) has two towers. One of them, topped by an elegantly powerful Gothic spire, is connected to a bell-turreted staircase tower by a footbridge. The other tower is a less ethereal.

This Renaissance **belfry**, adapted from the great Anglo-Norman towers to suit the new architectural style (it was begun in 1588 and completed in 1642), has a dome with lantern turrets. It was used as a prototype for a number of towers throughout Brittany. On sentry duty in the porch are the Apostles, ready to welcome visitors. The **sacristy** (1719) is dominated by a lanterned cupola and barrel vaulting.

Although the church is interesting, it is the **calvary** (c. 1555, restored in 1650) that is the real masterpiece in Pleyben.

The **monumental gateway** dates from 1725.

Pleyben.

Saint-Thégonnec.

SAINT-THÉGONNEC (Finistère)

The entrance to the close is a majestic **triumphal gateway** (1587) of four granite piles topped by lantern-turrets. The **calvary** (1610) was the last of the great calvaires to be built in the Léon Region. It has a plain base and three Crosses (the one in the centre, which bears a plethora of carvings of people, angels and horsemen, has two crossbars).

Nearby is the **funeral chapel** (or ossuary). It was built between 1676 and 1682. The decoration on the façade is an outstanding example of Breton Renaissance architecture. Inside, in the crypt, is a statue of the **Burial of Christ** (c.1699) comprising life-sized painted figures. Today, the chapel is the treasure house.

A Renaissance porch (1625) leads into the **church**. The belltower (1599-1610) has a proud Renaissance out-line. The belfry on the West gable is the oldest part of the church, dating from 1563.

The interior is somewhat disappointing, but it should be said that both nave and chancel were altered in the early 18th Century. The furnishings, however, are representative of the Counter-Reformation and are quite remarkable. The **pulpit** is worth a close look; it dates from 1683 and 1722.

The **Rosary Reredos** (1697) depicts a variety of scenes including St. Dominic and St. Catherine receiving the Rosary. The organ at the end of the nave is in a very high loft.

SIZUN (Finistère)

The masterpiece is probably the **triumphal gateway** (1588-1590). It is quite unique and comprises three semicircular arches. The platform, with its balustrade and lantern-turrets, stands on Corinthian columns. Above it is an altar and calvary.

The **ossuary** (1585-1588), which was also very carefully designed and built, has two levels. The upper section shows the Apostles on guard in niches separated by fluted pilasters. Lower down are small semicircular windows between which are some rather whimsical caryatids.

The octagonal spire (1723-1735) some 195 ft. high on **St. Sullian's Church** (16th to 18th Centuries) is not unlike the Kreizkêr in Saint-Pol. The great Flamboyant Gothic porch dates from the 16th Century.

Opposite: A religious procession, or pardon, in Le Folgoët.

Saint-Thégonnec.

THREE DAZZLING GOTHIC MASTERPIECES

LE FOLGOET (Finistère)

Le Folgoët Basilica lies one mile South of Lesneven. It has been a famous place of pilgrimage since the 15th Century and has one of the finest Flamboyant Gothic churches in the whole of Brittany.

The **basilica** was built between 1422 and 1460. On the outside of the basilica, note the North Tower. It is the only one to have been completed and is reminiscent of the ones on St. Peter's Church in Caen. Inside the basilica is a superb roodscreen made of kersantite.

KERNASCLÉDEN (Morbihan)

Notre-Dame Church in Kernascléden, an admirable Flamboyant Gothic monument, is a masterpiece of Breton architecture. The building is typical of the region

with its belfry above the gable-end, the wide South Wall with its huge rose window and two porches, and the great flat chevet containing the main window.

All over the building, the stone has been hollowed out, traceried to resemble lace, and scalloped. The decoration is equally subtle in the porches, one of which houses statues of the Apostles, and in the balustrades and piers with their niches, pinnacles and gargoyles. Inside, the Flamboyant Gothic groined arches support one of the few vaulted roofs in Brittany. But the really exceptional feature of Kernascléden is the **painting** which covers the arches in the North arm of the transept (angel-musicians and the Ascension) and, more especially, in the chancel (scenes from the lives of Mary and Jesus).

These paintings (it is a pity that they cannot be admired more closely) are an outstanding example of 15th-century French art. Those in the South arm of the transept are not as attractive but they are more surprising. Here, there are striking fragments, uncovered in 1912, of a danse macabre and a picture of Hell.

TRÉGUIER (Côtes-d'Armor)

St. Tugdual's Cathedral dates from the 14th and 15th Centuries. It is laid out in the shape of a Latin Cross and is 224 ft. long for a width of 57 ft. It has a rise of 58 ft. and the belltower (the slender traceried spire dates from the 18th Century) is 205 ft. tall. It is one of the most beautiful Gothic buildings anywhere in Brittany.

In the South arm of the transept stands a wood carving of St. Yves between a rich man and a pauper. In the chancel, note the 46 **Renaissance choir stalls** (1509) and the Flemish reredos (15th Century) depicting Christ's Passion. Be sure not to leave the cathedral without taking one last lingering look at the **nave**. Its architecture is unusually pure and the upsurge of the colonettes in the **transept crossing** is quite simply sublime.

The Flamboyant Gothic **cloisters** (1450-1479) form an admirable piece of lacework in stone. The galleries have 46 arcades divided into two trefoiled bays by a central pillar topped by a quatrefoil. In the cloisters, there are a number of tombs (including a recumbent figure dating from the 13th Century) and sculptures.

Top: The danse macabre in Kernascléden.
Bottom: Tréguier Cathedral.

Monasteries in Brittany

Landévennec (Finistère).

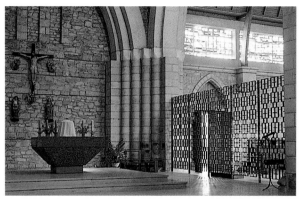

Saint-Michel de Kergonan.

Sainte-Anne de Kergonan.

BOQUEN (Côtes-d'Armor)

Bouquen Abbey in Plénée-Jugon was founded in 1137. During the French Revolution, it was used as a source of building stone.

It was reconstructed in 1936 after the arrival here of dom Alexis Presse (1883-1965) and his companions. Today, the 12th-century sanctuary has regained its original appearance. There are still some fine **capitals** left from the cloisters, of a design typical of Breton Romanesque architecture. The front of the **chapter house** has 13th-century ogival windows.

KERGONAN (Morbihan)

St. Anne's Benedictine Convent and St. Michael's Benedictine Abbey were built in Plouharnel in 1897-1898. They attract large numbers of people with a love of Gregorian chant.

LANDÉVENNEC (Finistère)

Surrounded by a rural landscape and woodland (beech, pines, chestnut and even palms) lying within a meander of the gentle R. Aulne before it flows out into the sea at Brest, the Landévennec Peninsula attracts visitors because of its mild climate and beautiful scenery.

In 913 A.D. the first monastery was destroyed by the Vikings. It was rebuilt and became one of Brittany's foremost spiritual and intellectual centres. For centuries, its sphere of influence was considerable but the French Revolution put a stop to all that. Thanks to the enthusiasm of Father Perrot, renewed interest began to be

Boquen.

Our Lady of Boquen.

shown in the abbey in 1935. In 1950, the Benedictines of Kerbénéat purchased Landévennec and decided to rebuild the monastery.

All that remain of the old **abbey** (on the site or in the museum) are a few pre-Romanesque features but most of the building dates from the 11th Century.

LANGONNET (Morbihan)

Langonnet **Abbey** stands on a hilltop above a wooded valley. Founded in 1136 A.D, the former Cistercian monastery is today occupied by the Fathers of the Holy Spirit. The buildings, which were reconstructed in the 17th and 18th Centuries, house a small colonial museum. The wonderful 13th-century chapter house from the original abbey can still be seen today.

LA MEILLERAYE-DE-BRETAGNE (Loire-Atlantique)

In La Meilleraye-de-Bretagne lies Meilleraye (or Melleray) **Abbey**, founded in the mid 12th Century by the Cistercians, but most of the present buildings date from the 18th and 19th Centuries.

The **abbey church**, open only during Sunday services, is classically austere. It has a 14th-century belfry.

TIMADEUC (Morbihan)

The Cistercian Abbey of Our Lady of Timadeuc was founded in 1841 in Bréhan near Rohan. The church dates from 1898 but most of the monastery buildings are more recent.

The Cistercians have had a community in Campénéac since 1953.

Langonnet.

The ruins of Landévennec. Overleaf: Landévennec Abbey.

Castles in Brittany

La Bourbansais (Ille-et-Vilaine).

Branféré.

Architecture in Brittany is not restricted to churches, chapels and abbeys, although it has to be said that religious architecture flourished here to an extent seldom seen anywhere else. A trip through the region soon reveals that the entire Armorican peninsula is also dotted with a large number of superb castles, most of them built in the Middle Ages and the Renaissance period.

In the Middle Ages, a network of high-towered fortresses was built along the region's Eastern borders (Vitré, Grand-Fougeray), in inland areas (Elven-Largoët, Tonquédec, Josselin) and along the coast (Saint-Malo, Fort-la-Latte, Hennebont, Concarneau, Pornic). Later, at the end of the 15th Century, new fortifications were built to withstand artillery attack (Guingamp, Nantes, Dinan) while the Louis XII style became fashionable in the interiors (Nantes, Josselin). Large, austere manorhouses decorated with a turret on the façade began to appear in the countryside.

At the end of the 16th Century and in the 17th, there was renewed enthusiasm for large castles with spacious square pavilions roofed in slate. The verticality of these more recent castles is created by an austere wall of granite devoid of any decoration (Kerjean, La Touche-Trébry, Coscro).

LA BOURBANSAIS (Ille-et-Vilaine)

The Château de la Bourbonsais in Pleugueneuc (Ille-et-Vilaine) stands at the end of an avenue of beech trees. The building, which is surrounded by formal gardens, consists of two wings set at right angles to each other. It is built in a number of different styles from a variety of periods (late 16th to 18th Centuries). The grounds are open to the public; they contain a **zoo**.

BRANFÉRÉ (Ille-et-Vilaine)

This 17th-century castle (which has been extensively restored) is best-known for its 50-hectare zoological **park**. It was a botanic garden in the 18th Century. Today, it has some 220 species of animal, including large colonies of coney, kangaroos, ibis and some twenty storks that have become perfectly acclimatized.

Combourg.

Elven.

Overleaf: Fort-la-Latte.

COMBOURG (Ille-et-Vilaine)

From Gustave Flaubert to Albert Camus, dozens of writers have come on a pilgrimage to Combourg. And all have gazed, with some emotion, at the mediaeval pile that is the castle overlooking the lake, for it was here that François-René de Chateaubriand spent part of his youth.

The castle was built in the 11th Century by the Bishop of Dol. The Moor's Tower is said to date, at least in part, from this period. The frontage and Crusader's Tower are 15th Century; the others date from the 14th. But the building underwent major restoration in the 19th Century, especially in the interior.

ELVEN-LARGOET (Morbihan)

The Elven Towers are the remains of the old Largoët Castle which was built, or rather rebuilt, in the late 15th Century. Lengths of curtain wall veiled by foliage connect the two towers to the fortified gateway (15th Century). The interior of the 15th-century Round Tower has been restored. The keep (late 14th Century), an enormous six-storey tower, has had its floors removed. The building is 143 ft. high, making it one of the tallest keeps in France. The 15th-century chapel lies in ruins.

FORT-LA-LATTE (Côtes-d'Armor)

The fort stands some 195 ft. above the English Channel to the East of Cap Fréhel on a small rocky island separated from the mainland by two gorges. This means that the fortress is virtually impregnable. Despite alteration in the late 17th Century carried out by Siméon Garanjeau to adapt the fort to the needs of the artillery of the day, it has survived up to the present time without any major changes to the original 13th and 14th-century structure. It has been restored by the Joüon des Longrais family who have owned the fortress since 1931.

GOULAINE (Loire-Atlantique)

To get to Goulaine Castle, you have to cross wide stretches of marshland. It is a real Loire Valley castle lost in the middle of the Nantes Region, built in the second half of the 15th Century by the de Goulaines to whom it still belongs.

Although it is not open to the public, you can still admire the rectangular tower entrance and the main building with the ornate dormer windows to either side of two magnificent staircase towers (15th Century).

LA HUNAUDAYE (Côtes-d'Armor)

This strategically important fortress (mainly late 14th and early 15th Century) in Plédéliac was once the mightiest and most impregnable castle in the whole Penthièvre area. The castle now lies in ruins but the polygonal outer wall is still a fine sight with its towers, walls and chimney bases.

La Hunaudaye.

Josselin.

JOSSELIN (Morbihan)

Built in the late 12th Century, extended in the 14th, and dismantled in the 17th, Josselin Castle was then restored in the 19th. Yet despite damage over the years, it still has an impressive, massive and yet subtle appearance when seen from the suburb of Sainte-Croix. The wall facing the river has three huge round towers, their bases cut straight into the rock. On the opposite side, the wall overlooking the main courtyard is extremely elegant, with a wealth of ornamentation. Probably the finest example of Louis XII architecture is Brittany, it looks like a piece of lace worked in stone, bordering the balustrades and casements of the uppermost windows with an exuberant display of pinnacles and colonnettes. The interior is also richly-decorated and includes a Doll Museum.

KERJEAN (Finistère)

Kerjean Castle in Saint-Vougay is a Classical Renaissance building (c.1540-1595) that is half-fortress, half-manorhouse. The Saint-Vougay road becomes a majestic beech-lined avenue that is at its most beautiful as the rays of the setting sun filter through the branches. It is then that the castle's defences stand out at the end of the avenue - walls 40 ft. thick, reinforced at all four corners by casemates, and a curtain wall.

Visitors can stroll though the grounds (Renaissance fountain), tour the castle, or visit the family apartments which are now a Museum of Breton Art and Furniture (16th and 17th Centuries).

OUDON (Loire-Atlantique)

Oudon, on the right bank of the Loire, is dominated by a **keep** that stands in the middle of the ruins of a 13th-century castle. The octagonal tower (105 ft. high) was built in the late 14th Century. To get to the top (from which there is a fine view of the valley), take the spiral staircase that runs up beside two huge empty rooms.

PORNIC (Loire-Atlantique)

According to Michael Jones, an expert in such matters, Pornic Castle is "one of the few mediaeval castles that actually stand on the coast". It was built in the 13th and 14th Centuries but was damaged during the Vendée Uprising and had to be restored in the 19th Century.

LA ROCHE-JAGU (Côtes-d'Armor)

A tree-lined avenue leads to the castle, built in Ploëzal at the beginning of the 15th Century at the top of the woo-

La Roche-Jagu.

Kerjean.

Les Rochers.

ded hill on the left bank of the Trieux. It is a granite stronghold with three towers incorporated into the wall. Note the decorated **chimneys on the gable** ends and the covered parapet walk on the second floor which served as an observation post overlooking the Trieux valley. The castle has become a cultural centre. It has recently been restored and belongs to the *département* of Côtes d'Armor.

LES ROCHERS (Ille-et-Vilaine)

Built in the 14th Century and altered in the 17th, this castle near Vitré has hardly changed at all since the time when the Marquise de Sévigné lived there. As you enter the courtyard, you will see the 18th-century outhouses. The castle lies to the left, capped by silvery slate roofs.

The castle is privately-owned but the chapel and **green chamber** i.e. the Marquise de Sévigné's bedroom, are open to the public. The various sections of the formal gardens laid out by André Le Nôtre still have the names that she gave them.

ROSANBO (Côtes-d'Armor)

Standing in the middle of formal **gardens**, the present castle (14th - 19th Centuries) in Lanvellec was built on the site of a fortress, on top of a huge rock high above the Bo Valley. It underwent alteration on several occasions and is now composite in style but most of the buildings date from the early 16th and late 17th Centuries. The East wing is Neo-Gothic (late 19th Century).

The rooms on the ground floor contain Breton and Italian Renaissance **furniture**. The **library** of books and archives put together by Claude Le Peletier, Colbert's successor in 1683, is housed in the modern part of the castle.

SUSCINIO (Morbihan)

This imposing fortress (13th-16th Centuries) built within the boundaries of Sarzeau a few yards from the Atlantic Ocean was one of the residences of the Dukes of Brittany.

The curtain walls, which once had eight towers (only seven remain), run round a vast courtyard. Over the centuries, the castle has been partially rebuilt. The East wall dates from the 14th Century; the North-East wall is 13th Century (and is the oldest part of the stronghold). New Tower to the North-West dates from the 15th Century.

The castle was bought by the *département* of Morbihan in 1965 and is now undergoing restoration with a view to using it as a museum.

TONQUÉDEC (Côtes-d'Armor)

Set on a rocky promontory overlooking the Léguer Valley, Tonquédec Castle must have been a fine sight when it was first completed in the early 15th Century. Today its majestic and romantic ruins stand in the midst of woodland. It is certainly one of the most striking feudal ruins in Brittany and the view from the top of its towers is very impressive.

Suscinio.

The 19th Century

The theatre in Rennes (1831).

By the 18th Century, the region's creative minds were slowly running short of original ideas. The king's architects and engineers in Brittany were firmly of the opinion that only Paris had buildings worthy of note and they therefore reproduced locally the architectural styles that had flourished in Versailles and the capital.

Soon, however, economic constraints and the introduction of town planning led to major projects such as a north-south road in Nantes, the canalisation of the R. Vilaine and the building of the quays in Rennes. The railway arrived with the laying of the Paris-Nantes line in 1851 followed by the Paris-Rennes line in 1857; this brought movement to the countryside. It was also at this period that the huge viaducts were built in Dinan (1845) and Morlaix (1865). The architectural style of the stations comes as something of a surprise in places such as Vitré, which has a Neo-Gothic castel built in 1855.

With very few exceptions, architectural designs made constant references to the past. Popular designs included the Neo-Gothic, the Neo-Classical, the Neo-Flamboyant and the Neo-Breton. The Neo-Gothic style in particular flourished with panache in the late18th and early 19th Centuries in the new urban districts in Nantes (Graslin Theatre in 1788, St. Nicholas' Church in 1844, chancel in the cathedral from 1840 onwards). Building began on the Palais du Commerce in Rennes in 1886; the theatre dates from 1846.

The first St. Vincent's High School in Rennes (now the Jean Macé High School, 1844) was built in the Italianate style. The vast Basilica of St. Anne d'Auray (1873) was built in the Neo-Renaissance style.

Among the architects who gained fame during this period were Jean-Baptiste Martenot, Joseph Bigot, Le Guerranic and Canon Daniel (he designed the Neo-Gothic church in Mûr-de-Bretagne). Another well-

Clisson.

known name was Arthur Regnault (1839-1932) whom we have to thank for the Neo-Breton style of the belfries on Notre-Dame Basilica in La Guerche and the church in Les Iffs, or the Romanesque-Byzantine style of the church in Corps-Nuds.

TWO OUTSTANDING BUILDING PROJECTS

CLISSON (Loire-Atlantique)

The town was entirely rebuilt in the Neo-Classical Italian style from 1798 onwards by the Cacault brothers. Its flat-roofed houses and umbrella pines have earned it the nickname "the French Tivoli". The **La Garenne-Lemot Park**, named after the sculptor who worked on the town's reconstruction with the Cacault brothers, dates from the same period. It lies between the rivers Sèvre and Maine, at the foot of a viaduct (1841). From outside the park, one can catch a glimpse of a few Neo-Classical buildings, particularly a Temple of Vesta and an imposing Roman villa.

PONTIVY (Morbihan)

In 1802, a decree promulgated by the Consuls indicated that the sub-prefecture of Morbihan was to undergo radical transformation. It was soon to be renamed Napoléonville, a name which it retained until 1814... and took again in 1815 during the One Hundred Days. It then used the name again during the days of the Second Empire, from 1852 to 1870. Napoleon Bonaparte's idea was to turn the town into an administrative and military centre so that the new national leadership would have a firm grip on the centre of Brittany where central authority was still being flouted. Situated at the junction of the

Pontivy, once called Napoléonville.

The Palais du Commerce in Rennes, which houses a post office.

Nantes-Brest Canal (then in the planning stage) and the R. Blavet which was made navigable as far as Lorient, Napoléonville was, in the Emperor's mind at least, destined to become a hub of road and rail networks.

Pontivy has two districts, each very different in appearance. To the North is the mediaeval town; to the South, the imperial town. In the centre of the imperial town is a vast parade ground known as La Plaine. It is flanked to North and South by the Law Courts and the Sub-Prefecture, standing opposite each other, while to the West, near the R. Blavet are the monumental Clisson Barracks. The Joesph-Loth High School was opened in 1806 but the present buildings date mainly from 1885. The public, vernacular and military buildings all form part of a coherent architectural design that was well-suited to the new layout and was intended to underline the power of central government. The buildings constitute a rare example of early 19th-century town planning. Note St. Joseph's Church (1869), a fine example of Neo-Gothic architecture.

Pontivy.

The 20th Century

The new Law Courts (1984) in Rennes.

The traditions of the 19th Century lasted into the 1920's, with everybody turning to the past or to foreign countries in a search for architectural or aesthetic inspiration. With the exception of a very few buildings, the days of major projects such as castles and cathedrals were past. Building work became more individual, with a plethora of private townhouses and residences that looked like stage sets for operettas. Some of the frontages were still decorated with reminders of Rococo architecture (*Ouest-Eclair* building, rue du Pré-Botté, Rennes, 1916) and on the walls of townhouses, the Mannerist style of decoration remained fashionable. A few Italianate buildings (the new St. Vincent's High School, Rennes, 1912) and pseudo-Oriental styles (Aussant House, boulevard de Sévigné, Rennes, 1910) distinguished themselves from the rest but they were nevertheless based on the same desire to reproduce styles and models from elsewhere.

When the *Neo-Gothic* style came into fashion, regional traditions came back to the fore in the guise of an original Neo-Breton form of architecture drawing its inspiration from the 15th-17th Centuries. Today, draughtsmen's imagination is fired by the juxtaposition of geometric volumes produced by the large slate roofs, as they search for a truly regional architecture adapted to contemporary society. Unfortunately, the Neo-Breton movement is usually bogged down in demands for that most caricatural and derisive of all architectural styles — the modern detached house.

Rennes : St. Vincent's High School (1912) seen from the Thabor Gardens.

Brest Harbour.

The bombing raids of the Second World War laid waste to entire towns (Lorient, Brest, Saint-Nazaire, Saint-Malo) and their reconstruction has not always been a success. Today, although the expansion of urban districts and industrial estates, people's passion for holiday homes, and the erection of the farm buildings that are vital for modern production methods, have all helped the region's economic situation, they have by no means improved it from an artistic and aesthetic point of view. On the outskirts of the large towns, new neighbourhoods display their insipid faded walls of concrete, while in the suburbs there is row upon row of white pebble-dashed bungalows. And aggressively-designed blocks of flats at the water's edge have spoilt quite exceptional beauty spots for ever.

It has to said, though, that the town centres have been the scene of extensive urban planning and improvement programmes over the past few decades (Brest, Nantes, Rennes etc.). Modern art has flourished here and there (e.g. the "Degré" by Nissim Merkado in Rennes-Atalante). Many of the buildings remain mediocre but some of them are unusual, elegant and functional (Crédit Agricole in Vannes, 1976; new Law Courts in Rennes, 1982). One particularly fine example of modern architecture at its best is the Assurances Générales de France building in Rennes (1981) which is unfortunate in that it is surrounded by concrete on all sides. On the coast and in inland Brittany, however, many breathtaking beauty spots have been destroyed by concrete jungles and villas built in a decidedly repetitive style. In town centres and on the outskirts of towns, thousands of advertising hoardings spoil the countryside a little more each day. There is no doubt that Brittany will have a lot to do to protect its inherent beauty and its cultural identity.

Armor, the Coastal Strip

The Coast of Love.

The Breton coastline, which is sometimes called Armor, is rocky and indented, with characteristic estuaries. Indeed, most of the towns are built at the point furthest upstream reached by the tides (Dinan on the R. Rance, Lannion on the R. Léguer, Morlaix on the R. Dossen, Quimper on the R. Odet, and Hennebont on the R. Blavet). These estuaries, which are known as "rias" or "abers", are the result of the flooding of valleys by the sea.

However, there is a marked difference between the North coast with its high cliffs (Cap Fréhel) and narrow rias, and the South coast which is lower-lying and less indented. Its rias are wider, opening onto the sea, and islands such as the Glénans, Groix and Belle-Ile ring its vast bays. Between these two coastlines, capes and headlands jut out into the sea, separated from each other by Brest Harbour and the Bay of Douarnenez. They include the Pointe Saint-Mathieu, the Crozon Peninsula, and Cap Sizun (Pointe de Raz) with the offshore islands of Ushant and Sein.

Brittany's seabased geographical situation provides the very purest of maritime climates. The winter is mild

Crozon (Finistère).

and wet. In summer, temperatures are moderate, although they become higher as one nears the R. Loire. The air is invigorating and full of ozone. The climate is particularly suitable for shrubs; they grow on slopes around fields and beside the high-banked paths in woodlands. They give the landscape the characteristic colour so beloved of artists and writers.

Opposite: Pointe de Brézellec (Finistère).

Cancale (Ille-et-Vilaine).

In Armor (or Arvor, in Breton), employment is linked directly or indirectly to the sea. The majority of the population lives along a coastal strip 12 miles wide. Thanks to the mild climate, the production of early vegetables provides the impetus for a go-ahead agricultural community, while tourism is the main industry in the many seaside resorts, making Brittany the second most popular tourist venue in France. Armor is home to two-thirds of all French fishermen, with harbours ranging in size from tiny sheltered moorings with their brightly-coloured craft to the big industrial fishing harbours like Lorient and Concarneau (the 2nd and 3rd largest in France). Moreover, urban-based industries are also concentrated in the coastal strip, the main towns being Brest, Lorient, and more especially Nantes.

Concarneau.

APPOINTMENTS WITH THE SEA

LA BAULE (LOIRE-ATLANTIQUE)

Of all the towns along the Atlantic coast, La Baule is probably the only one that can compete with the resorts on the Riviera. Thousands of tourists flock here every summer to admire "the most beautiful beach in Europe" with its 5- mile crescent of fine sand, or to spend a few days in the villas scattered amidst the pine trees.

CONCARNEAU (Finistère)

Concarneau is France's foremost tuna fish port. Since 1905, the town has been staging the **Blue Nets Festival** every year at the end of August. It is one of the most popular events in Brittany.

Opposite: The walled town in Concarneau.

La Baule.

Morgat in the Crozon Peninsula.

Opposite: Pointe de Pen-Hir near Camaret.
Overleaf: Dinard.

In the centuries when Christianity was spreading throughout Brittany, a daughter-house of Landévennec Abbey was founded on the island that is now the walled town. A ring of fortifications was first built in the 13th-14th Centuries, rebuilt from 1451-1477, and finally repaired and completed by Vauban in the 17th Century.

The **Walled Town** should be seen from the outside, from the Place Jean-Jaurès for example. The ramparts run round an island some 400 yds. long. To the left are a **belfry** and clocktower which fit in well with the other buildings.

CROZON PENINSULA (Finistère)

The Crozon Peninsula has an exceptionally large number of grandiose beauty spots in a comparatively small area. The trident jutting out into the Atlantic Ocean between the Brest roadstead to the North and the Baie de Douarnenez to the South is a succession of striking landscapes of cliffs, creeks and rocks worn away into strange shapes by the waves. If you are looking for the secretive, untamed side of Brittany, this may well be the place to find it.

Morgat to the South is a seaside resort. A boat trip to the Morgat Caves along the cliffs is a pleasant outing. The "gateway" or **Pointe de la Chaise** (Beg-ar-Gador)

to the South-East is a picturesque spot. Beyond it are the headlands called Saint-Hernot (cf. Armorica Park), Dolmen and Rostudel.

The D225 road leads to the **Cap de la Chèvre**, a mighty sandstone headland with cliffs indented by caves. Between this headland and the Pointe de Dinan are the most attractive landscapes and seaviews in the peninsula, with successions of cliffs, coves, creeks, beaches and capes. The beach at **Lost-Marc'h** (the Breton word for the plant known as mare's tail) is especially charming. Further North, the **"Château" de Dinan** and its headland are connected by two natural archways. Nearby, the **Grottes des Korrigans** (Fairy Grottoes) are remarkable for their colours and their high roofs, but they are difficult to get to. Visitors should not attempt to go there without a guide.

DINARD (Ille-et-Vilaine)

The town has remained faithful to its vocation as an international tourist centre but it has succeeded in diversifying its attractions (Val-Pirée Equestrian Centre, golf course, tennis courts, and conference centre). Dinard has a superb Protestant church (1871) and a small **Museum** near Notre-Dame Church. But it is best known for the wonderful

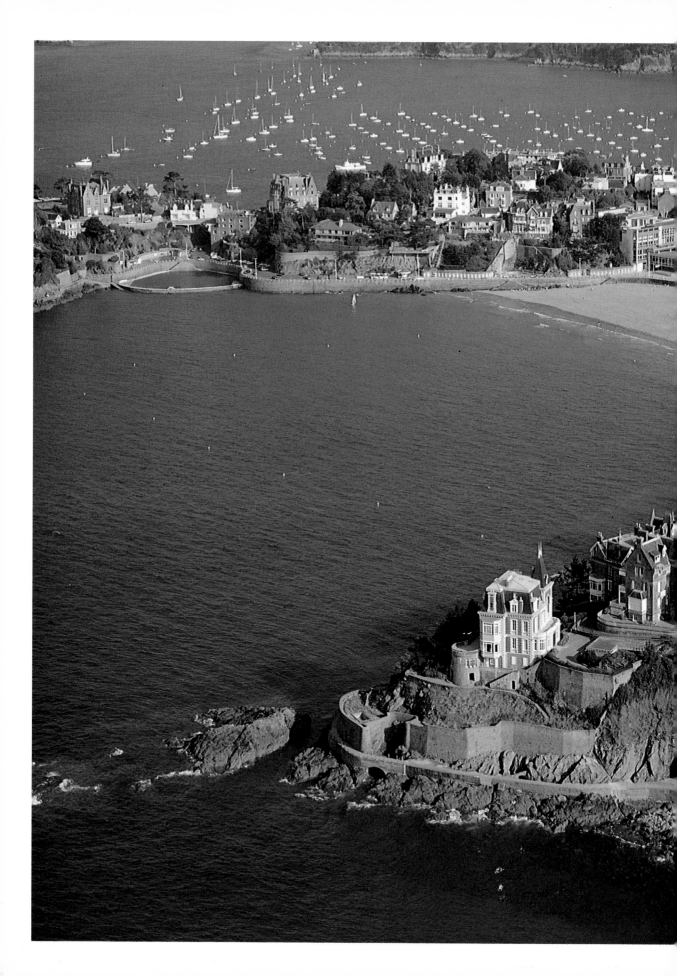

Erquy.

Douarnenez.

footpaths leading from its beaches. The largest beach is on the North side. It is the **Plage de l'Ecluse**, which lies between the Pointe de la Malouine and the Pointe du Moulinet. From there, a footpath along the shore leads to the **Plage de la Prieuré** to the South-East (opposite Saint-Malo). It takes you past the casino, conference centre and aquarium to the Promenade du Clair-de-Lune where, sheltered from the winds, there is an amazing variety of Mediterranean vegetation (palm trees, agaves, and eucalyptus).

The resort has been easier to reach since the building of the dam across the R.Rance (1960-1966) and the **tidal power station**.

DOUARNENEZ (Finistère)

Douarnenez remains one of the foremost fishing ports in France. The town, though, is better-known as the European capital of maritime heritage thanks to the **Port-Musée**, a floating and land-based museum opened in 1993. Tradition has it that, beneath the waves of Douarnenez Bay, slumbers the town of Ys, the Atlantide of Brittany.

A puffin.

Erquy.

ERQUY (Côtes-d'Armor)

Erquy is one of the main shellfishing ports in France (large catches of scallops in particular are landed here). It is also a bustling seaside resort. Its **headland**, consisting mainly of pink sandstone, is outstandingly beautiful with moors and sheer cliffs (max. height 221 ft.).

FRÉHEL (Côtes-d'Armor)

This is one of the most spectacular places in the whole of Northern Brittany. It is also the highest point on the Emerald Coast. Porphyry and red sandstone cliffs

tower some 225 ft. above the waters of the English Channel.

There is a natural sanctuary for migratory birds on the pink sandstone rocks in the small and large **Fauconnière** to the East of the headland.

Two **lighthouses** look out over the headland and sea. The older (and smaller) of the two was brought into service in the 17th Century. The present lighthouse was inaugurated in 1950. In fine weather its light shines over some 62 miles and from the level of the lamp itself the view extends right along the coast and, occasionally, over to the Channel islands.

Cap Fréhel.

MORBIHAN GULF

With its 125 miles of coastline and its 39 sq. miles of water dotted with islands, the Morbihan Gulf has numerous walks and cruises on offer. Yet sailing is not without its dangers. Despite appearances, the Gulf is not calm water and it has several very strong currents. It is a world of its own, enjoying an unusually mild climate. Tens of thousands of migratory birds spend the winter here and oyster-farming is one of the main industries.

The Gulf comprises dozens of islands but most of them are fairly small and only two have borough status viz. Ile-aux-Moines and Arz.

From Larmor-Baden, you can take a boat trip to the **island of Gavrinis** where there are some magnificent prehistoric monuments in a setting dating from the Late Stone Age.

Arz.

PLOUMANAC'H (Côtes-d'Armor)

Ploumanac'h in Perros-Guirec is famous for its amazing piles of old rose-coloured **rocks**. These large blocks of stone have taken on the most fantastic shapes.

Rocks in Ploumanac'h on the Pink Granite Coast.

Arz.

The best way of discovering Ploumanac'h is to follow the coast in an East-West direction. From the end of the coastal footpath from Perros-Guirec, you will see the rocky outcrop of Pors Rolland then the "devil's castle", and further North the beautiful **Pointe de Squewel**.

From there, go on to **Pors-Kamor cove** and Ploumanac'h **lighthouse** from which there is a panoramic view of the Sept-Iles Archipelago in the North. The main group of rocks that have been sculpted by the elements are to the South-West. Napoleon's hat, for example, is near **St. Guirec Beach**.

PORT-LOUIS (Morbihan)

Until the 17th Century, this small town with a population of 3,000, situated on the headland controlling the entrance to Lorient Harbour, was a fortress and a major fishing port.

The **citadel** (1590-1636), surrounded by the sea that pounds its granite bastions, stands guard opposite Lorient Sound. It is the finest (and perfectly-preserved) example of late 16th- and early 17th-century military architecture in France. Today, the fortress includes the **French East India Company Museum** and the Atlantic Museum.

Port-Louis.

LE POULIGUEN (Loire-Atlantique)

Le Pouliguen is a charming little port with tree-lined avenues of old whitewashed fishermen's cottages.

Take the coast road along to the Pointe de Pen Château - the shore bristles with cliffs and rocks. Just before the headland, facing the sea, is the **Chapel of St. Anne and St. Julian** (16th Century).

POINTE DU RAZ (Finistère)

The long rocky promontory that is the Pointe du Raz, in **Plogoff**, descends to sea level in a series of steps and stairs. Eight miles offshore beyond the La Vieille Lighthouse is the island of Sein with its circlet of reefs. The pass, or race, is one of the most dangerous in Europe.

For a walk around the headland (alt. 234 ft.), you should be accompanied by an official guide. There are striking views of the sea's erosion of the rocky outcrop. The waves rush in, underwashing the crest, sinking, and frothing up in a headily-deep depression called the **"Hell of Plogoff"** where the souls of the departed can be heard moaning.

Between the two headlands at each end of **Cap Sizun** lies the **Baie des Trépassés** (literally "Bay of the Dead") which has long symbolised the point of departure for the hereafter.

Hôtel de l'Iroise, on the Pointe du Raz.

SAILLÉ (Loire-Atlantique)

The village of Saillé, a mile from Guérande, stands on a former rocky island in the heart of the salt marshes. For generations past, salt has been the main source of income for the inhabitants who still exploit the pans today.

Of all the villages on the peninsula, Saillé is the one that has best preserved its traditional character. It still has the lime-washed **houses** that are the usual accommodation for workers, and the slate roofs of the past. The salters' costume is one of the most unusual in Brittany.

Pointe du Raz.

Batz.

THE MAGIC OF THE BRETON ISLANDS

BATZ (Finistère)

Located two nautical miles off Roscoff (15 mins. away by boat), the island stretches over 2 1/2 miles from West to East and is half-a-mile wide on average. Although it is low-lying, it protects Roscoff from northerly winds. The South coast has a particularly mild climate and early vegetables are grown there. The islanders also make a living from seaweed, fishing and tourism. To the South-east is a **Colonial Garden** and, nearby, the ruins of a **Romanesque chapel** (10th Century). In the same area, there is also a prehistoric graveyard and dolmen (made Christian in the 13th Century by the addition of a calvary). The North coast is wilder and more rugged.

The island is superb walking territory. To the west you can visit the **lighthouse** (211 steps) built at the highest point along the coastline (114 ft.).

BELLE-ILE-EN-MER (Morbihan)

Belle-Ile is the largest of all the Breton islands, 10 miles long, 3 - 6 miles wide, with 50 miles of coastline comprising cliffs, creeks and beaches. It is a block of hard rock sloping gently down to sea level on the North coast, while presenting a wild inhospitable face to the open sea.

The island has four towns and villages - Le Palais, Bangor, Locmaria, and Sauzon.

Le Palais, the island's main town, is dominated by a citadel built in the mid 16th Century, extended by the de Gondis and further fortified by Fouquet and Vauban who visited the island in 1682. Today, it houses a museum. From there, visitors can go to the Pointe de Taillefer from which there is a panoramic view of the Morbihan coast. **Sauzon**, in the North-West, lies at the entrance to a winding valley. From the Pointe des Poulains, which is

Overleaf: Belle-Ile-en Mer.

Batz.

Belle-Ile-en-Mer: The Apothecary Grotto.

The **Apothecary Grotto** to the South-West of Sauzon was once the haunt of cormorants; the rows of nests in the crags of the rock were reminiscent of the jars in a chemist's shop. On stormy days, the sea rushes through a sort of natural tunnel. Further South lies Port-Donant Beach, flanked by cliffs. The **Port-Coton** Needles are pyramids of rock worn to a point by the sea. The Talut Cave is accessible at low tide.

BRÉHAT (Côtes-d'Armor)

Bréhat is a pile of heavy pink granite rock worn smooth by natural erosion, but the mild climate and vegetation are also reminiscent of a Mediterranean island. Rainfall is low; the clouds usually drift on past. The flowers are as colourful and abundant as in the South of France. There are eucalyptus trees, oleanders, maritime pines, mimosa, myrtle, fig trees and almond trees. There, however, the similarities cease, for not far away, frequent storms and squalls lash the coastline's red rocks. Although the interior is a tranquil place, the Northern part of the island is absolutely wild. Thousands

connected to the island by a sandbank, there is a good view of the strange-shaped rocks of the so-called Wild Coast formed by the West end of the island. The Pointe du Vieux-Château is a bird sanctuary (seamews, cormorants, herring gulls); it was a fortified headland in the Iron Age.

Bréhat.

of stones seem to have been scattered over the heath where the clumps of heather are scorched by the wind. Bréhat is an island of contrasts.

Two miles long and one mile wide with an area of 309 hectares, Bréhat lives in a world of its own. There is no pollution, for motor vehicles are banned. Birds converge naturally on the island. There are curlews, sea-mews, cormorants, herring gulls etc.

Bréhat has to be discovered gradually, with its squat thatched-roof cottages, its more modern bungalows covered with wisteria, its narrow paths and its thousand and one creeks. The village lies to the North of Port-Clos where the launches disembark their passengers. Standing near **St. Michael's Chapel** (half-a-mile to the West of the village), the view extends right over the island and the Kerpont, the narrow stretch of water separating Bréhat and the **island of Béniguet** which is also inhabited. The scenery is especially beautiful at sunset. **La Corderie Bay** is the island's real harbour; indeed, up to and including the 19th Century, it was a harbour of some importance.

The lighthouse (**phare de Paon**) 2 miles North-east of the village stands high above a mass of tumbled rocks.

GLÉNAN ARCHIPELAGO (Finistère)

The Glénan Archipelago is made up of some 10 main islands and several smaller ones. Its marl and sand are still put to occasional use but today the name of Glénan more frequently conjures up pictures of the sailing school which was opened on the islands of Penfret, Drenneg, Cigogne and Bananec in 1948.

In summer, the Ile Saint-Nicolas is the one that draws the biggest crowds. Boatload upon boatload of holidaymakers come ashore here and there is a sub-aqua centre on the island. The others (Geoteg, Kignenek, Cigogne with its old fort, and Le Loc'h) attract yachtsmen, scientists from Concarneau's maritime research centre, and ornithologists.

GROIX (Morbihan)

The island is approximately 5 miles long and 1 mile wide. It is a vast, almost flat, plateau protected by towering cliffs, especially on the South coast. From the impressive

The island of Saint-Nicolas in the Glénan Archipelago.

Groix Harbour.

Top to Bottom:
A coastal path on Groix.
Hoëdic.
Houat.

Left: The Glénan Sailing School.

inlet called Trou d'Enfer (Hell Hole) to Port-Saint-Nicolas, a small forked fjord, the coast should be visited on foot. Fine sandy beaches stretch along the East coast, providing visitors with calm and shelter. The local sailors used to specialise in tunny-fishing; more than 300 of them used to go in search of tuna aboard their ketches between 1880 and 1950. Today, this type of fishing has died out altogether.

Since 1952, a life-sized tuna-fish has topped the weather vane in the village of Loctudy. *"A cockerel is all right for farmers!"* say the seafarers. A Folk Museum was opened in Port-Tudy in 1984.

HOUAT AND HOEDIC (Morbihan)

There is no doubt about it : in Breton, *"houad"* means "duck" and *"hoadig"* means "duckling", and a comparison of the relative sizes of the "twin" islands seems to lend weight to this explanation.

Today, Houat has a few restaurants and pancake-houses and a couple of hotels, which is not bad at all considering that, in 1909, the Conty guide-book specified *"Visitors may sleep in the rectory"*. Unlike other islands, Houat has not pinned all its hopes on tourism. The concrete jungle merchants may complain, but at least the island has been able to preserve much of its traditional character.

Houat is 3 miles long and slightly over 3/4 mile wide. The highest point on the island just tops 100 ft. The plateau is used for farming but over the last ten years people have turned to lobster-breeding.

The rustic church is dedicated to St. Gildas, as is the harbour. He lived on Houat in the 6th Century. A memorial stands at the entrance to the cemetery. The island's houses are low, and some of them are whitewashed.

Hoëdic is only 2 miles long and 1/2 mile wide. Yet it had a larger population than Houat at the turn of the century. Since then, though, numbers have declined steadily.

OUESSANT (ISLAND OF USHANT) (Finistère)

Four miles long and almost three miles wide, Ushant (called "Enez-Eussa" in Breton, from the Gallic "Uxisana" meaning "the highest") is in a world of its own. Most of the houses are single-storey cottages with five windows and one door, wisely turning their backs on the wind. It is true that there is some modern housing, probably too much of it in fact, hence the authorities' decision to include Ushant in the Armorica Regional Park. Here and there are white or black sheep, all of them short and stocky so that they are better-protected from the wind.

To visit the island, you should go as the mood takes you, but be sure not to miss the extraordinary **North-**

Ushant.

West coast between the Baie de Béninou and the **Créac'h Lighthouse**, one of Ushant's main tourist attractions. The lighthouse (just over 1 mile from the village of Lampaul) was opened in 1862 but not until 1939 did it become one of the most powerful lights in the world.

Ushant.

The Quai des Français Libres on the Island of Sein. Overleaf: the Island of Sein.

The **Pointe du Pern** not far away (only 2 miles from the village) has rocks shaped like animals. In fact, the island itself is shaped like a crab's pincer.

To the North-East is the **Pointe du Stiff** (from which there is another interesting view). Nor should you miss the **Pointe de Pen-al-Lann** to the East or the **Pointe de Pen-ar-Roc'h** to the South-East. And if you are lucky, you may even spot a colony of grey seals during one of your walks around the island.

The main village is **Lampaul** which has a number of old houses. In Nion-Huella, 1 mile away, are the two **Centres of Ushant Technology and Traditions**.

The **island of Molène**, the usual stopover between Ushant and the mainland, is much smaller. In fact, it is only 3/4 mile long and slightly more than 1/2 mile wide.

SEIN (Finistère)

The landscape is bare, the ground flat, the vegetation stunted. The average altitude scarcely exceeds 5 ft. which explains why Sein was almost submerged beneath the waves on several occasions.

To visit the island, go where the will takes you. The alleys round the harbour sometimes have strange names (the Street of the Impudent Cockerel, or Go-up-to-heaven Street). None of them is more than a yard or two wide.

From the top of the lighthouse on the Western side of the island, there is a view across the **Sein Causeway**, a line of reefs that run some 6 miles out to sea. At the tip is the **Ar-Men Lighthouse**, one of the most inhospitable on the coast. It took almost 15 years to complete (1867-1881).

LES SEPT-ILES (Côtes-d'Armor)

The Sept-Iles Archipelago offshore from Perros-Guirec enjoyed enormous publicity in 1967 but it was of a type that the islands would have preferred to do without. It was then that an oil slick gradually covered the Pink Granite Coast and the archipelago that lies off-shore from it. It was a catastrophe for the bird sanctuary that had been on the island since 1912.

From East to West, the archipelago contains the islands of **Rouzic** (the best-known of them all), **Malban, Bono**, l'**Ile-aux-Moines**, l'**Ile-Plate** and its tiny neigh-bour l'**Ile-aux-Rats**, les **Cerfs**, and, to the North of Bono, les **Costans**. That makes eight rather than the seven islands in the name and the archipelago also includes other islets and rocks.

Nowadays, the Sept-Iles Archipelago is a nature reserve managed by the French society for the protection of birds *(Ligue française pour la protection des oiseaux)*. It is still the only seabird reserve of its kind in France.

It is forbidden to land on the islands (except on l'Ile-aux-Moines) but you can enjoy a boat trip round them leaving from Perros-Guirec.

Inland Brittany

The scenery in inland Brittany, or Argoat (literally the "land of woods"), is never monotonous. Some areas are hilly, although the overall average altitude is unimpressive. Two such upland chains have been given the name "mountains"; running from West to East, they consist of sandstone and crystalline rocks which jut out from the somewhat sparse vegetation. In the West, they are known as the ***monts d'Arrée*** (the highest point, at Tuchen-ar-Gador, has an altitude of 1,250 ft.) which run eastward to become ***the Méné Moors*** (Bel-Air near Montcontour lies at an altitude of 1,100 ft.). To the South stand the ***Montagnes Noires***, preceded in the West by rocky outcrops such as Menez-Hom (1,070 ft.), and Roche-du-Feu (710 ft.). The final peak in the range is at Toul-Laeron (1,060 ft.). To the South-West, the mountains run down to the ***Lanvaux Moors***.

There are also low-lying areas. In the West, the ***Châteaulin Basin*** is hemmed in by the Monts d'Arrée and the Montagnes Noires, but the ***Rennes Basin*** forms a wide depression stretching from the Channel down to the Loire Valley. To the South of Rennes, it is broken up by

a series of hills and valleys, all running perpendicular to the R. Vilaine which winds through a narrow valley between cliffs (cf. Pléchâtel, Langon).

This area is very sparsely-populated. Nature is unfriendly in the area, with a predominance of moorland

Opposite: Monts d'Arrée.

Saint-Cadou (Finistère).

and woods. It is a mainly agricultural region which, over the last ten years, has begun to look towards factory farming using the most up-to-date animal husbandry techniques. In the centre of Brittany (Châteaulin, Landerneau, Guingamp, Saint-Brieuc, Loudéac, Rennes) the countryside is studded with long modern buildings in which cows, pigs and poultry are raised. Brittany leads the rest of France in this sector. This type of farming is backed up by a large food-processing industry (animal foodstuffs, slaughterhouses, etc.).

Inland Brittany, though, is also (and perhaps more particularly, for visitors) a fascinating area full of places of interest that are often all too little-known.

LA BRIERE (Loire-Atlantique)

This vast stretch of marshland (6,700 hectares) is one of the last places in Brittany in which man and Nature live at peace with each other.

The area appears to be somewhat introverted; it is criss-crossed by reedy canals and covered by inhospitable looking swamps. The best time to come is winter when the water reaches its maximum depth. It is easy then to drift slowly through the Brière in a "blin" (a flat-bottomed boat) and venture into the labyrinthine network of canals that drain the Grande Brière. But whatever the season, make sure you are accompanied by a local.

The Brière Marshes.

The Brière has scarcely changed at all in hundreds of years. Some of the marshes have been drained and turned into grazing land, and a few roads now run through the area. But the real Brière still exists.

Most of the villages are built on small outcrops of granite on which the houses are sheltered from the untrustworthy waters of the marshes. However, the locals never build their houses far from the canal in which they moor their flat-bottomed punts. A number of tiny villages are dotted across the Brière, clusters of low whitewashed houses with thatched roofs. They include **Saint-Joachim**, the main town, **Crossac**, and **Saint-Malo de Guersac** (which has a zoo and lock-keeper's house open to the public).

In 1970, the Brière became a regional park with an area of some 40,000 hectares (the Grande-Brière itself covers an area of 6,700 hectares).

The **island of Fédrun** to the South-West of Saint-Joachim is probably the best preserved traditional village. It is a homogenous, very well-protected place with low, white, thatched cottages. It was chosen as the Park's administrative centre, and also boasts the Bride's House and a traditional Briéron cottage (furnished as in days gone by). The other two islands, **Pendille** and **Mazun**, are also worth a visit.

FOREST OF BROCÉLIANDE (PAIMPONT)

With its 7,000 hectares of forest, fourteen lakes and thousands of legends, not to mention the several castles of which it is so proud, Paimpont, or to give it its other name, Brocéliande, figures largely in Breton tales of fantasy and imagination.

Les Forges-de-Paimpont is a picturesque village on the edge of the forest with cottages, mills and 17th-century fountains. The foundries existed as far back as the Renaissance when local iron was smelted here. They reached their peal of prosperity in the 17th and 18th Centuries.

Paimpont (3 miles North-West of Les Forges) lies beside a lake and is far and away the largest village in Ille-et-Vilaine (its area exceeds 11,000 hectares). It is worth paying a visit to the **abbey church** (13th Century with major 15th- and 17th-century alterations). It comprises a

Brocéliande.

small number of Romanesque features. The **abbey buildings** (17th Century) have a certain air of grandeur.

Going Eastwards from Paimpont, you will come to the **Pas-du-Houx Lake**, the largest stretch of water in the forest. In the distance is **Brocéliande Manor**.

La **Haute-Forêt**, 2 miles North-West of Paimpont, is the most interesting area of all, for the forest climbs to an altitude of 829 ft. here. This is the highest spot in the *département* of Ille-et-Vilaine.

Comper Castle is still further North, 2 miles East of **Concoret**. Dismantled in the 16th Century and burnt to the ground during the French Revolution, the castle was not finally rebuilt until 1870. This is one of the most popular places in the forest. The castle stands in the midst of the moorland, its walls reflected in the waters of a lake.

From Comper, take the Concoret road and head South-West towards Tréhorenteuc. On your way, stop at the hamlet of Folle-Pensée just past La Saudrais, and walk down to the **Barenton Fountain** (one mile away). If you pour water from the spring onto **Merlin's Steps** (Perron de Merlin), you will conjure up a storm of wind, rain, hail, thunder and lightning. Then a ray of sunshine will calm the tempest and a huge flock of birds will fill the skies. Well, you can always try anyway.

Forest paths lead to the **Valley of No Return** (Val-sans-Retour) or the **Valley of the Faithless Lovers** (Val-des-Faux-Amants).

Among the additional places of interest are :

- The tiny church in **Tréhorenteuc**, to the West, a masterpiece of fantasy and imagination.

- **Trécesson Castle** to the South-West (early 15th Century).

CHAMPEAUX (Ille-et-Vilaine)

Champeaux is a small village off the main tourist routes, yet it is an architectural gem with a square surrounded by granite houses, a well (1601) and a church. Rebuilt c. 1430, it is one of the most interesting churches in Upper Brittany.

The North chapel leading off the nave (15th Century) is built of stone; the one on the South side (16th Century) is made of wood. It includes a vivid **Pentecostal Window** (1529) and a canopied altar, also dating from the Renaissance period.

In the **chancel** (1522-1550), there is a **Crucifixion Window** (early 16th Century) and a **tomb** nicknamed "the nuptial bedchamber". This monument, which is over 22 ft. high, was built in honour of Guy III d'Espinay who died in 1553, and his wife, Louise de Goulaine, who passed away fourteen years later. It is a unique two-storey mausoleum of white stone and red and black marble, with recumbent figures of Guy III and his wife, both of them completely naked.

CHATEAUBRIANT (Loire-Atlantique)

The town lies on a low hill surrounded by woodland and lakes. Apparently, it was built on the very spot where

A path in the Brocéliande Forest.

one of the Gallic tribes, the Cadeti, had their settlement. It was in the 11th Century that the lord of the manor, Briant, (from whom the town gets its name) built the first fortress. The present **castle** has two parts: the 11th-century Vieux-Château, or Old Castle (which underwent subsequent alteration) and the Château-Neuf, or New Castle. Of Briant's original buildings, there remains the square keep which is reached by way of a 13th-century barbican. From the main courtyard, the difference between the mediaeval building and the **Renaissance palace** (1533-1539) is quite striking.

Near the castle, there are several mediaeval houses, for example in the rue de Couéré, which has three 15th-century dwellings, including the "Angel's House".

St. Nicholas' Church in the town centre dates from the 19th Century but **St.-Jean-de-Béré** is an 11th and 12th-century building (altered in the 17th Century). It lies to the North-West near the Rennes road.

CHATELAUDREN (Côtes-d'Armor)

The old capital of the Goëlo region houses one of Brittany's artistic treasures. The Chapel of **Our Lady of the Knoll** (early 15th Century, with later alterations) possesses very rare **paintings on wood** dating from the end of the 15th Century. On the arch above the chancel, there are 96 paintings representing scenes from the Bible; in the South chapel, another 32 pictures illustrate the life of St. Fiacre and St. Margaret. Although they

Châteaubriant.

lack the subtlety of the frescoes in Kernascléden, the paintings in Châtelaudren are nevertheless remarkable. Thanks to modern lighting, it is now possible to admire the paintings in detail.

FOUGERES (Ille-et-Vilaine)

Situated on the borders of Normandy and Maine, Fougères was an important fortress in the Middle Ages for it overlooked one of the roads into Brittany. Today, Fougères is a quiet sub-prefecture which has been famous since the 19th Century for its shoe factories.

Fougères.

The best view of the old mediaeval town is to be had from the public park, the **Place aux Arbres**. In the North-West corner of the park are the ruins of a square tower known as the **Popinjay Tower** (14th Century).

St. Leonard's Church not far from the park has a Flamboyant Gothic West Front dating only from 1880 and three aisles built in the 15th and 16th Centuries. The nearby **Town Hall** dates from 1535. It has a 12th-century vaulted chamber and some attractive fireplaces. In the Rue Nationale, the **Museum** devoted to the painter Emmanuel de La Villéon (1858-1944) is in the only house in the town with a porch.

The upper town has a number of fine houses (e.g. no. 18 rue Chateaubriand). The **belfry** dates from 1387.

The Rue de la Fourchette leads to Notre-Dame Gate flanked by two machicolated towers then to **St. Sulpice's Church** with its pointed slate-roofed belltower. It was built in the 15th Century in the Flamboyant Gothic style and al-tered in the 16th and 18th Centuries. In the arms of the transept are two fine altars with granite screens carved into the walls. On the left-hand reredos is a statue of **Our Lady of the Marshes** (said to date from the 11th Century).

Access to the **castle** is by way of the square tower called La Haye-Saint-Hilaire (a rare example of 13th-century fortifications). The keep was razed to the ground in 1166, but thirteen of the towers in the outer wall are still standing, all built between the 12th and 15th Centuries. They are all visible from the parapet walk running round the main enclosure.

HUELGOAT (Finistère)

In Huelgoat, myth is more important than reality. Its forest (dotted with piles of rocks and rushing streams) and its historical and prehistoric remains all give it a very particular meaning for Bretons.

Huelgoat.

The usual visit to the natural beauty spots in Huelgoat starts from the lake and more or less follows the course of the R. Argent. The piles of rocks or their strange positions have all been given evocative names like the Mill, the Devil's Cave, the Shaking Rock (a huge pile of stone which answers questions by swaying back and forth), the Virgin Mary's household, the Mushroom etc. A few hundred yards into the forest to the North of the Carhaix road, at the end of Lovers' Lane *(Sentier des Amoureux)*, is Artus' Grotto where King Arthur of the Bretons sleeps.

LANRIVAIN (Côtes-d'Armor)

Lying off the beaten tourist track in the very heart of inland Brittany, Lanrivain nestles in a truly rustic setting. The cemetery has a 15th-century ossuary but it is the calvary (16th Century) which is of particular interest: note the thieves on their crosses.

Half-a-mile away is the **Chapel of Our Lady of Le Guiaudet** (late 17th Century), which has been a place of pilgrimage since 1692. The electric **carillon** (16 bells) plays two Breton hymn tunes.

The **Toul-Goulic Gorge** (2 miles from Lanrivain) is a picturesque spot. The R. Blavet disappears from view for some 100 yds. beneath the pile of rounded granite rocks; it can be heard rumbling and roaring down below.

MENEZ-BRÉ (Côtes-d'Armor)

There are two moments at which one can capture the real atmosphere of Menez-Bré (alt. 981 ft.) in Pédernec - in clear, bright weather when the horizon seems to stretch into infinity, and during the very fiercest of storms when gusts of wind and rain beat against the lone mountain.

St. Hervé's Chapel which stands at the top of the rise used to be much frequented by those suffering from scalp disorders (although Menez-Bré itself is bald).

MONTAGNES NOIRES (LES)

This is perhaps the true Brittany; it is the most secretive part in any case. Yet it is less attractive to tourists, who, instead of discovering things for themselves, prefer to follow sign-posted and busy paths and roads. The Montagnes Noires are, in fact, rolling hills. The highest point is at **Roc'h Toul-Laeron** (i.e. the thieves' cave, alt. 1,060 ft.) in Spézet to the North of Gourin. The "Black Mountains" are therefore much lower than the Monts d'Arrée.

Like these other hills though, they consist of hard sandstone and quartzite. The extensive forests which once covered the Montagnes Noires (hence their name perhaps) have now disappeared; only the Laz Forest and a few minor woodlands still exist today.

Monts d'Arrée.

MONTS D'ARRÉE (Finistère)

At 1,250 ft. **Tuchenn-ar-Gador** (i.e. the Mound of the Throne, rather stupidly taken into French as the Toussaines Peak) is the highest hill in the whole of Brittany. It is closely followed by the **Roc'h Trévézel** (1,245 ft.), Mont Saint-Michel de Brasparts (1,238 ft.) and the Roc'h Trédudon (1,196 ft.).

The mountains form a natural geographical feature where the R. Ellez has its source. The deserted, even unreal appearance of this timeless landscape has given the place a special meaning. The bottom of the corrie is formed by **yeun Ellez**, i.e. the Ellez Marshes. They have become a lake whose waters were used, from 1966 to 1985, in the cooling system of a nuclear power station. Yet, in spite of everything, this isolated region has lost none of its inherent strangeness. Will-o'-the-wisps are still to be seen here. Standing guard over the souls of the departed who wander through the marshes is the chapel at the top of the **Mont Saint-Michel-de-Brasparts**, in Saint-Rivoal. The Saint-Michel farmstead in the village houses arts and crafts exhibitions.

The **Monts d'Arrée Folk Museum** housed in the Kerouat Mills in **Commana** was opened in the 1970's. It includes the upper mill (c. 1615), the lower mill (1812), a number of buildings dating from the 18th and 19th Centuries, and several bread ovens.

The Folk Museum is part of the **Armorica Regional Park** (it includes 33 towns and villages, the département and the City of Brest). The Park Centre, the **Ménez-Meur Estate**, lies in Hanvec, just over 5 miles from Saint-Rivoal.

QUELVEN (Morbihan)

The village of Guern has a church that is of no particular interest, while the remarkable **Notre-Dame Chapel** in the hamlet of Quelven is one of inland Brittany's leading spiritual centres. It stands on a hilltop overlooking the whole area and is an impressive sight that is visible from several miles away.

The chapel was probably built in the late 15th Century but it had to be restored and enlarged in the 16th.

Inside, note the ogival arching in the chancel and transept, the corbels in the nave, two 16th-century stained glass windows, a frigate donated as a votive offering in the 18th Century, the lord's gallery, and an alabaster bas-relief (the Coronation of the Virgin Mary) dating from the 16th Century. Among the statues is a **group** comprising **St. George** and St. Hervé and his wolf but the finest piece of all is a **front-opening statue** of the Virgin Mary (15th Century).

QUÉNÉCAN FOREST (Morbihan)

The forest that stretches northwards to the shores of Guerlédan Lake has numerous places of interest. The hydro-electric dam was built between 1923 and 1929. It is 222 yds. long and 146 ft. high. The church in **Saint-Aignan**, which underwent major restoration between 1893 and 1895, dates from the mid 16th Century and has a wonderful Rod of Jesse. Above the hamlet stands St. Tréphine's Chapel (1897).

A forestry road to the South of Saint-Aignan leads deep into the woodland. Many of the place names in the 2,300-hectare forest have some connection with the foundries that were among the oldest in the area. The forest abounds in beauty spots such as Breuil-du-Chêne half-a-mile to the East of Sainte-Brigitte. And a boat trip on the lake will take you through the Blavet Gorge.

St. George slaying the dragon, in Quelven.

SAINT-HERBOT (Finistère)

The attractive rural community of Saint-Herbot in Plonévez-du-Faou is named after St. Herbot, patron saint of horned animals. The Gothic **chapel** (14th - 16th Centuries) is a superb building. Its most noteworthy feature is the main portal dating from 1516.

The Saint-Herbot area is one of the most beautiful parts of Inland Brittany which, although or perhaps because it is more difficult to reach, is more delightful than better-known and more-frequented beauty spots.

SAINT-SULPICE-DES-LANDES (Loire-Atlantique)

The recently-restored church in the old village (a Romanesque building) has some very rare early 15th-century **frescoes**. Some of the paintings are quite remarkable e.g. the angel musicians, and the hanging of Judas Iscariot on which Satan is seen drawing the soul of the Apostle out of his belly.

La **Motte-Glain Castle** in La Chapelle-Glain to the North near the Châteaubriant-Angers road is a late 15th and early 16th-century building. It houses a small **Hunting Museum**.

SPÉZET (Finistère)

The **Chapel of Our Lady of Le Crann** is one of the few rural churches to have kept its original furnishings and, more importantly, its stained glass windows. On top of the building (1532-1535) is a Renaissance lantern-turret which can be reached from the outside by a flight of steps cut into the pitch of the roof. The stained **glass windows** (1545-1550) show German (Rhineland) and Italian influences.

Quénécan Forest.

The stained glass window in Notre-Dame-du-Crann in Spezet.

Trévarez.

All along the **Aulne Canal** runs a towpath that constitutes one of the best walks in the neighbourhood.

TRÉVAREZ (Finistère)

At the edge of the Laz Forest is the remarkable Trévarez **Estate** (180 hectares) in Saint-Goazec which was purchased by the département in 1968. It comprises :

— the old manorhouse (and 106 hectares of land) which has been made into an experimental farm.

— the new castle built between 1894 and 1906 on a rock overlooking the Aulne Valley. The Neo-Gothic design is based on the castle in Courances (Essonne). In 1944, it was the target of a RAF air raid, and was later ransacked and pillaged. It is presently undergoing restoration.

The 75-hectare park includes an extensive forest and almost 8 miles of footpaths and avenues. Hundreds of varieties of rhododendrons, camelias, azaleas, and hydrangeas make up an outstanding collection of flowering shrubs. In the **archaeological museum** at the end of the luxurious stable block, are exhibits relating to recent discoveries made at Saint-Thois and Saint-Goazec. The **castle houses** a variety of events right through the year. The prehistoric graveyard (Bronze Age), which was uncovered in Saint-Goazec in 1977, was reconstructed in Trévarez using the shale slabs that once formed 19 stone coffins.

Towns Worth a Visit

Saint-Malo.

BREST (Finistère)

Brest stands on a quite exceptional spot. Built on a plateau, the town overlooks the huge natural harbour, or "roadstead", which can take the largest ships and even atomic submarines. Accessible only by a narrow strait (1 1/2 miles at its widest point), it is easy to defend. This explains Brest's rôle as a military and maritime base for approximately 2,000 years (the Romans built mighty fortifications here). It also explains why, during the Second World War, the Allies' planes pounded away at the naval base until it was totally destroyed.

There is almost nothing left of the old town. The **castle** houses the Regional Shipping Office while the **Tanguy Tower** (16th Century but much restored) is now a museum. A solitary 17th-century gateway stands in the middle of the modern Square du Commandant l'Herminier.

Océanopolis, the sea life centre near the Moulin-Blanc yachting marina on the Rue de Kerbriant, was opened in 1989. It is a scientific and technical research centre devoted solely to the marine environment and has the largest open-air aquaria in Europe.

DINAN (Côtes-d'Armor)

Dinan is one of France's most attractive walled towns. Its geographical setting is quite exceptional. Instead of nestling on the valley floor like Morlaix, most of Dinan's urban development has been on the hillside. Thus the town overlooks the 225 ft. drop down to the R. Rance. The most fascinating view of the town with its viaduct, ramparts, towers and belfries is to be had from the hill at Lanvallay, on the Rennes road.

Start your visit from the Place du Champ, and walk up the Rue Sainte-Claire to the Place du Théâtre. The pillared house on the left of the square is the 16th-century **Keratry Residence**. A few yards away, the **Jacobins Theatre** stands on the site of a convent which was founded in 1224; a few remains of the original building can be seen inside.

Nearby is the rue de l'Horloge with its 15th and 16th-century houses and, more especially its late 14th-century **belfry** some 97 ft. high.

Turn back and take the Rue de Léhon which leads to the **St. Louis Gate** (1620), the most recent of the town's

The Brest '92 Festival.

gateways. From the other side, there is a general view of the "castle". Dinan had been without a fortress for one hundred years when, in the late 14th Century, the **Duchess Anne's Tower** was built. Today, it houses a very interesting museum. The Port du Guichet (14th Century) forms the entrance to the castle. The town walls can only be visited in their entirety during the **Ramparts' Festival**.

At the foot of the keep is the **Promenade des Petits Fossés**, which leads to the narrow alleyway known as the Trou-au-Chat. From there, take the **Rue de la Cordonnerie** on the left; it is bordered by 15th-century houses with oriel windows. The street runs down to the Place des Merciers, on which stands **Old Mother Pourcel's House**, containing a remarkable 16th-century wooden staircase.

The Place des Cordeliers still has a few arcaded houses (16th Century) and the 15th-century gateway to the **Franciscan Friary**, founded c. 1245. There is nothing left of the original Franciscan sanctuary and most of the buildings were completed in the 15th Century. The most noteworthy examples of this period are the **cloisters**, the courtyard (Capitole Tower) and the **chapter house**.

Dinan: the street leading to the harbour.

Dinan Castle.

Nearby, at no.4 in the Grand'Rue, is the remarkable six-sided turret on the **Hôtel de Plouër** (early 16th Century but with some 18th-century additions).

Beyond the house is **St. Malo's Church** on which work started in 1489. It is built in the Flamboyant Gothic style but was not completed until 1865. On the South side is a double Renaissance doorway.

From there, turn back to the **Place de l'Apport** with its exceptional group of arcaded houses, all of which have been subject to restoration.

On the left on the way down the Rue Haute-Voie is a Renaissance doorway; it opens onto the courtyard of the **Beaumanoir Residence** (1535).

The narrow Rue de la Larderie leads to **St. Saviour's Basilica**. Every century from the Romanesque period onwards has left its mark on this church. The lower part of the façade (note the projecting sculptures of winged creatures above the modern tympanum) and the South side wall date from the 12th Century. The church was largely rebuilt in the late 15th and 16th Centuries but has never really been completed (there is one side aisle missing). The interior is dark and oppressive but not devoid of interest. Note the font (12th Century), the **Evangelists' Window** (15th Century), the Rosary Reredos and the nearby Empire-period cenotaph which has contained the heart of Bertrand Du Guesclin since 1810, and the huge canopied High Altar (18th Century).

The **English Gardens** lie beyond the church near the old ramparts overlooking the river flowing through its enchanted valley.

A **viaduct** (812 ft. long and 130 ft. high) has linked Dinan and Lanvallay since 1852. From the English Gardens, take the Rue du Rempart, the Rue Michel and the alleyway beyond it; this will bring you to the **Rue du Jerzual** and its continuation, the **Rue du Petit-Port**, which run down to the harbour.

DOL-DE-BRETAGNE (Ille-et-Vilaine)

The architects of **St. Samson's Cathedral** (13th Century) were strongly influenced by the Norman Gothic style and also, to a lesser extent, by English Gothic architecture. It is one of the most outstanding historic monuments in Brittany. The West Front, with its 12th-century rectangular door (once part of the Romanesque cathedral) is flanked by two towers. The one on the left was begun in the 16th Century but never completed. The other dates from the 15th Century and its campanile was erected in the 17th Century.

The nave has three storeys i.e. the great arches supported by pillars that are themselves strengthened by four secondary columns, the triforium and the clerestory with a gallery at its base. The English-style chancel ends in a flat chevet. The great stained **glass window** (late 13th Century) is one of the oldest in Brittany.

Opposite: Dol Cathedral.
Dinan: The Ramparts Festival.

The **Grand'Rue des Stuarts** has several noteworthy old houses. At no.15 the **House of Plaids** with its beautiful arcades is almost the only example of Romanesque vernacular architecture (12th Century) in Brittany. At no.18, the House of the Green Cross dates from the 12th-16th Centuries; the **Guillotière House** at no. 27 is 15th-century. No. 32 is the **Chartier Courtyard** (15th Century) while no. 33 consists of a fine 17th-century townhouse. There is a Local **History Museum** at no. 4 Place de la Cathédrale. North from the town is Mont-Dol which is also worth a visit.

GUINGAMP (Côtes-d'Armor)

The town was founded by craftsmen and traders who put up fortifications to protect it against invasion by the Vikings and Normans. Tréguier and Lézardrieux had already been pillaged. As well as being a fortress, Guingamp was also a ducal seat in the 14th and 15th Centuries when the Blessed Charles of Blois and Pierre II lived there.

The **Place du Centre** and the nearby streets all contain 16th-century half-timbered houses or 17th-century granite dwellings. Several of the doors date from the Breton Renaissance period, including the one in the courtyard of the "Relais du Roy" which opens onto a grand stone staircase. At the top end of the Place du Centre stands a beautiful Italianate fountain.

The **Basilica of Our Lady of Assistance** *(Notre-Dame de Bon Secours)* is built in a composite style. Originally, the church was the chapel for the castle but in the

Locronan.

The Italianate fountain in Guingamp.

11th Century it became the church of a newly-created parish. It was rebuilt in the 14th and 15th Century in the Gothic style.

Between the two towers on the West front is a Renaissance doorway with two bays beneath a huge window. The tympanum and arching are richly decorated. Above each door are statues of two human figures. The North side is Gothic but the South side and front are Renaissance. Behind the porch on the North side is an **outside shrine** containing the statue of Our Lady of Assistance, one of the few black Virgins in France. The annual procession to Our Lady of Assistance takes place on the Saturday evening before the first Sunday in July.

The **Town Hall** (1699), a former Augustinian convent, has an impressive façade embellished by a Baroque chapel (1709) which is a typical example of the architecture of the Counter-Reformation in Brittany. Not far away to the South on the banks of the R. Trieux, are the remains of the **ramparts** and the **castle** (mid 15th-century) which was demolished in 1626 on the orders of Cardinal Richelieu.

LOCRONAN (Finistère)

There is no doubt that Locronan boasts the most attractive collection of houses in Lower Brittany.

In the centre of the evenly-paved **square** stands a well. Round about is a unique group of freestone houses dating from the 16th and 17th Centuries when the canvas industry ensured the town's prosperity. The village has a small museum.

Standing side by side are the intercommunicating **St. Ronan's Church** (15th Century) and the 15th- and 16th-century **Pénity Chapel**.

The church is built in a uniform style. Building began in 1420 and was completed in 1480 with the inclusion of the main window. Inside, there is a stone-vaulted roof, a rarity in Brittany. Because of the lie of the land, the church is built on two levels. The ten medallions round the **pulpit** (1707) tell the story of St. Ronan. In the right-hand side aisle, there is an example of late mediaeval wood carving in the striking statue of Christ awaiting his torturers. Other statues represent St. Ronan, St. Corentin, and St. Christopher. The **Rosary Reredos** dates from 1668. The sacristy houses the church's treasure.

Eaten away by a green slime caused by the underground springs below the building, the Pénity Chapel houses a large stone polychrome statue of **The Lamentation of Mary** (1517) and **St. Ronan's Tomb** on which the saint is seen dressed in his vestments and wearing a mitre. The kersantite monument dates from the mid 15th Century.

At the end of a steeply-sloping alley that runs uphill from the North end of the square stands the **Chapel of Our Lady of Good News** (Notre-Dame de Bonne Nouvelle, 15th to 17th Centuries), which has a small Renaissance lantern turret. Inside, there is a 16th-century carving of Christ being laid in the tomb.

Every six years (1995, 2001 etc.), an almost unique procession is held in Locronan, the **Grand Troménie**, probably a deformation of "tro minic'hi" or "tour of the monastery lands". It covers almost 8 miles and people process through the countryside along the route supposedly followed by the saint every week. The ceremony begins on a Sunday morning in July with the saluting of the banners. In the afternoon, the solemn procession gets underway to the sound of drums. As for the **Minor Troménie**, it is held every year, on the second Sunday in July, unless there is to be a Grand Troménie. The route covers approximately 3 miles.

LORIENT (Morbihan)

Sheltered at the end of the harbour into which flow the rivers Scorff and Blavet, Lorient was not originally really part of Brittany. It was in 1666 that a royal decree created the town of L'Orient. Shipyards were set up and the town soon became the headquarters of the French East India Company.

Little is left of the old town of Lorient - two Louis XV pavilions designed by Gabriel for the East India Company at the entrance to the naval dockyard, the 18th-century Discovery Tower and, below it, the two Admiralty powder mills, one of which houses a naval museum. Not far away on the Quai des Indes, a few houses of the French East India Company line the docks.

Lorient.

The town was rebuilt after the terrible air raids that razed it to the ground between 1941 and the surrender of the German garrison on 8th May 1945. The centre was redesigned on a rather austere geometric pattern, but in line with tradition the house fronts are still sparkling white. Lorient, a town undergoing massive economic expansion at the present time, has regular flights to and from Paris at the Lann-Bihoué Airport (the new terminal building dates from 1982).

Every year during the first week in August, a major **Inter-Celtic Festival** is held in Lorient. An Academy of Traditional Breton Music, Song, Dance and Sport was opened in 1981 near Ploemeur.

MORLAIX (Finistère)

There are numerous traces of the old town (once the third largest in Brittany) but the appearance of the 16th- and 17th-century city has altered considerably. The **viaduct** above the town, which seems to crush the houses below, dates from 1863. It is 191 ft. high and 923 ft. long.

To visit the town, leave from the Place des Otages in the centre. To the North is the viaduct; to the South the town hall (1845). Near the viaduct on the East side of the square is a flight of stone steps leading to **St. Melaine's Church**. It is built in the Flamboyant Gothic style and has a modern lantern tower, a fine 17th-century organ, old furnishings, and a rare statue of St. Rose of Lima, the patron saint of the New World.

To the left of the steps, note the Hôtel du Parc (Breton Renaissance). Take the **Rue Ange-de-Guernisac** behind the church; it is lined with corbelled houses built of local stone (granite and blue schist). From the Place de Viarmes, head for the Place des Jacobins, not by way of the very busy Rue d'Aiguillon but via the picturesque Rue du Fil. If you are a good walker, you can climb the steps in the Venelle des Fontaines and follow the Rue Sainte-Marthe up to Carmel. The Carmelite fountain backs onto the former front of the chapel. On the Place des Jacobins is the former Dominican church, now a **museum** after having been used as a barracks.

Port-Louis.

Behind the Dominican convent, you might like to take a stroll along the picturesque Allée du Poan-Ben where the R. Jarlot flows in the open air. When you get to the Paris road, turn right into the Rue des Bouchers and go on to **St. Matthew's Church**. All that remains of the old building is the large 16th-century tower.

From the church, go down the Rue du Mur to the Place des Halles which is lined with **old houses** (including Queen Anne's House). Most of them have "lanterns", i.e. the spiral staircase inside is lit by a bay window or lantern.

NANTES (Loire-Atlantique)

Situated in a zone that attracts much through traffic, at the confluence of the Loire, Erdre and Sèvre, the history of Nantes is rich in misfortunes and adversity. Its apparently uneasy maritime situation astride Brittany and Vendée, and not far from the Paris Basin via the R. Loire, has made it the largest city in Western France with a superb artistic and cultural heritage.

Historical fluke has resulted in the two most interesting sections of the town being quite separate. To the East is a small mediaeval city with the cathedral and the castle; to the West is a quite remarkable group of 18th-century buildings.

The **castle** is probably the one monument which has played the largest part in the town's development and fame. It was the residence of the Dukes of Brittany and the setting for numerous marriages and historical treaties. It is surrounded by a wide moat, now mainly laid out as gardens. The main entrance, in the Rue des Etats, is flanked by two mighty towers known as the **Doe's Foot Tower** and the **Bakery Tower** (15th Century), each of which has slit windows and window bars. On the other side of the castle, overlooking the Place de la Duchesse-Anne, the enormous **Horseshoe Tower** is connected to the **River Tower** by a curtain wall.

Opposite: Morlaix.

Nantes.

In the castle courtyard are more varied and elegant buildings, but all have one thing in common i.e. magnificent dormer windows with arched pediments. Near the entrance, there is a **wrought-iron** well dating from the late 15th Century. Opposite the well is a large four-storey building decorated with finely-traceried dormer windows, like lacework, in the Flamboyant Gothic style; further along is the **Golden Crown Tower**. The **old keep** is all that remains of the original castle (1207).

Inside the castle are three museums: the **Museum of Decorative Arts**, the **Naval Museum** (still known as the Salorges Museum) and the **Traditional Arts and Crafts Museum**. The third one, in the main apartments, is particularly worth a visit; it houses a large collection of local costumes, furniture and paintings.

From the castle it is only a short step to **St. Peter's Cathedral**. Take the Rue Mathelin-Rodier which leads directly to the parvis (Place Saint-Pierre). The cathedral was founded in the 4th Century, but it was not until the early years of the 15th Century that Mathelin Rodier drew up the plans of the Gothic cathedral as we see it today, a Flamboyant building showing absolute purity of line. The church is unusual in that it is built of white stone rather than of granite.

The West Front is interesting for its five doors and for the high quality of the sculptures which decorate the three central portals. The lower part of the **nave** is a masterpiece of elegance and sobriety with its moulded pillars rising to the arches above (122 ft.) in a line unbroken by capitals. Most remarkable of all is the superb **Tomb of François II** (1502-1507) and of his wife Margaret of Foix. The chancel was completed in the 19th Century. A **Romanesque crypt** was discovered beneath the South side of the chancel in 1886. The recent restoration work gave an opportunity to include the magnificent **stained glass windows** made by Anne Lechevalier and Jean Le Moal.

To the North of the cathedral is the slender outline of **St. Peter's Gate**. The various sections date from quite different periods. The present gate, which is built on

Opposite: Nantes seen from the air.

Nantes: A statue personifying the R. Loire on the Place Royale.

Nantes: Quai de la Fosse.

The Ducal Castle in Nantes.

Gallo-Roman foundations, dates from the 15th Century. A few yards from the cathedral (to the South) is **La Psalette**, built in 1502.

In contrast to the mediaeval town and dominated by the chevet of the cathedral, the Cours **Saint-Pierre** and Cours **Saint-André** run from the R. Erdre to the castle; they are shady esplanades with 18th-century town houses on each side. Their regularity is broken by the elegant **Place du Maréchal-Foch** over which a statue of Louis XVI stands guard at the top of a column that was rebuilt in 1926. From the cathedral, it is possible to go straight to the Town Hall via the Rue du Maréchal-Leclerc. The **town hall** consists of three buildings from the 17th Century, all in varying styles. From here, the Rue Saint-Jean and the Rue Juesseau lead to the County Buildings (préfecture), a classically designed symmetrical construction dating from 1763.

On the other side of the **Cours des Cinquante-Otages**, the backbone of the town, is the West end of Nantes built mainly in the 18th Century to plans by the architect Mathurin Crucy.

The Rue d'Orléans leads from the Cours des Cinquante-Otages to the **Place Royal**, one of the main attractions in this part of the town. It was designed by Mathurin Crucy in the late 18th Century but had to be almost entirely rebuilt after the Second World War. To the North-West stands **St. Nicholas' Church** (1844), an excellent example of the Neo-Gothic style. In the centre of the square is the Loire Fountain, which was sculpted by Driollet (1865). Take the **Rue Crébillon** on the West side of the square; it is one of the busiest thoroughfares in the town. If you do not stop for a look at the strange **Pommeraye Arcade** (19th Century) which leads off the Rue Crébillon, you will quickly reach the **Place Graslin** and its **theatre** (1788), with tall Corinthian columns decorating the façade. To the West of the square is the quiet **Cours Cambronne** (18th Century).

The **Quai de la Fosse** runs along the banks of the Loire and Nantes Harbour (the fourth or fifth largest in France if combined with Donges and Saint-Nazaire). To get to the quayside, take the Rue Voltaire, the Rue Do-

Nantes: Place du Commerce.

brée then one of the roads on your left. There are still some 18th-century houses along the quay, built by local shipowners. The buildings have preserved their austerity and their ornate balconies, especially at no. 86 (**Hôtel Darbré**), no. 70 (the former **East India Company Offices**), and no. 17 (a Louis XV style house with attractive wrought-iron balconies and carved bas-reliefs). No. 24 houses the superb **media library** (library, record library and its main attraction, a museum of printing).

Feydeau Island also has some luxurious residences especially in the Rue Kervegan. The Charron (1727) and Vellestreux Residences overlook the Place de la Petite-Hollande at the West end of the island.

The contemporary period has also provided the town with some large building complexes. The **Brittany Tower** seems somewhat aggressive in the midst of 18th-century Nantes, but the new Foreign Office and Sports Hall on **Beaulieu Island** are better suited to their surroundings. The old **Tobacco Factory** near the railway station has been turned into an Arts Centre.

In addition to the museums in the castle, Nantes has an interesting **Art Gallery** at 10 rue Georges-Clemenceau. Then there is the **Dobrée Museum** on the Place Jean-V in which one of the rooms houses an exhibition on the Royalist Insurrection, the **Jules Verne Museum** at 3 rue de l'Hermitage, the **Natural History Museum** in Rue Voltaire, and the **Doll Museum** on boulevard Saint-Aignan, to name but a few.

QUIMPER (Finistère)

The capital of Cornouaille is one of Britany's brightest gems, set in a beautiful ring of hills and dales. This *"charming little place"*, as Flaubert put it, lies a few miles inland from the sea at the confluence of the rivers Steir, Jet and Odet.

St. Corentin's Cathedral stands on the site of a former Romanesque church, and its construction lasted from the 13th to the 19th Centuries. Its spires, for example, were built in 1855 and were inspired by the ones in Pont-Croix. The twin towers (mid 15th Century) were part of the Anglo-Norman tradition that was so widespread in Brittany. The equestrian statue of King Gradlon (1858) on the platform was based on an earlier statue that was destroyed by revolutionaries in 1793.

Although relatively small (299 ft. in length), the cathedral is a fine example of Gothic architecture as developed in Brittany. The great spans with their luxurious moulding are evidence of the influence exerted by Normandy's architects. The chancel (1240-c.1287) is not in line with the nave, probably because the builders were anxious to incorporate the Victory Chapel into the 13th-century sanctuary.

The remains of the **ramparts** beside the cathedral indicate that this was once a walled town.

The old Bishop's Palace built by the Rohan family in 1508 (beside the cathedral) houses the Breton Museum which has some remarkable exhibits.

Not far from the cathedral is the **St. Francis covered market**. It is a convincing example of contemporary architecture (the rafters are built in the shape of an upturned hull).

On the other side of the square, the delightful **Art Gallery** (1872) is of major interest. It has paintings, sketches and engravings from the 16th to 20th Centuries.

A stroll through old Quimper should not be confined to the **Rue Kéréon** (i.e. Shoemaker's Street) opposite the cathedral. You really have to wander at will, for the town has more atmosphere than specific tourist attractions. Cross the footbridges and walk along the quays on an autumn evening and smell the scent of the chestnut trees. Go into the labyrinth of streets and squares that bear such evocative names. In the **Rue du Guéaudet,** the "house of heads" is said to show some of the pickpockets of the day. The narrow **Venelle St. Nicolas** has a flight of steps halfway up it. The finest house in Quimper stands in the **Rue du Sallé**.

The Rue Kéréon leads to the **Terre-au-Duc** which, unlike the town within the walls (episcopal land) was governed by the Dukes of Brittany.

At the foot of **Mount Frugy** (which towers some 227 ft. above the town), the **Allées de Locmaria** lead to the suburb of the same name, stronghold of the local glazed earthenware in-

Opposite: Quimper Cathedral.

Quimper.

dustry. In 1690, a ceramics expert from Provence, J-B. Bousquet, settled in Locmaria. There is a **Faïence Museum** on the Bénodet road, and the Kéraluc potteries (Rue de la Troménie) are also open to the public. It is at the foot of Mount Frugy that the Cornouaille Folk Festival is held every July.

Notre-Dame Church is the oldest monument in Quimper. The Romanesque nave dates from the first half of the 11th Century; the chancel, transept and tower are 12th Century.

RENNES (Ille-et-Vilaine)

The historical centre of Rennes is a juxtaposition, within a confined space, of two very different urban layouts. To the West and East of a checkerboard group of streets and squares flanked by regularly-proportioned buildings, are alleyways dodging between old houses. Until the 18th Century, Rennes was a town of large timbered cob houses and winding streets. Then, on 23rd December 1720, a fire broke out that was to burn for six days and destroy the

entire town centre. A wide-scale rebuilding project (as befitted the political capital of the region) was ordered by the King. The work lasted from 1723 to 1760.

The best place to start your visit is the **Museum** (1845 - 1855) on the Quai Emile Zola in the centre of the town, only a few yards from the Kléber car park. The **Museum of Brittany** presents the region's history, everyday objects and the lifestyle of its people from prehistoric times to the present day.

The **Art Gallery** (*musée des Beaux-Arts*) houses a number of treasures including the priceless painting of *The Newborn* by Georges de la Tour (1593-1652).

Behind the museum, in the Rue du Capitaine-Dreyfus, **All Saints' Church** (*église des Toussaints*, 1624-1651) is the chapel of the former Jesuit college which trained Brittany's ruling classes in the days before the French Revolution. The great 17th-century **reredos** had an enormous influence on Breton religious art. One hundred yards away, at no. 34 Rue Vasselot, there is a quite

Rennes: Place du Champ-Jacquet.

Place des Lices.

exceptional reminder of the 17th Century viz. an **outside wooden staircase**.

Come back to the Rue Dreyfus and cross the river by the Saint-Germain Footbridge then turn right along the Quai Chateaubriand towards the Kléber car park. On the North side of the R.Vilaine, you will see **St. George's Palace** (17th Century), a former royal Benedictine convent. Halfway up the hill is the **Rue Saint-Georges** which serves as a reminder of the architecture of Rennes before the fire of 1720.

Close by, at the foot of the rue Derval, is **St. Germain's Church**. It is built mainly in the Flamboyant Gothic style.

There is a striking contrast when you first catch sight of the beautiful **Place du Parlement de Bretagne**. The former Place Royale, designed by Jacques Gabriel, is the finest piece of architecture in the town, with its splendid apartments (1725).

The **Palace of the Parliament** of Brittany (1618-1655) on the North side of the square was designed by a local architect named Germain Gaultier, but the front was designed by Salomon de Brosse, the architect who designed the Luxembourg Palace in Paris. This architectural masterpiece was badly damaged by fire in February 1994.

The Rue de Brilhac in the South-West corner of the square leads to the **Town Hall** (1734-1762), a Baroque building designed by J-A. Gabriel, Louis XV's chief architect. On the opposite side of the square is the **theatre** (1831), a fine example of the Neo-Palladian style.

The Rue de l'Hermine to the right of the town hall and the Rue Du Guesclin beyond it lead to **St. Saviour's Basilica** (1703-1725) which stands on the square of the same name.

After visiting the church, turn right along the Rue de Montfort, the Place du Calvaire, then the **Rue du Chapitre**. This is the Western end of Rennes, which escaped damage in the fire of 1720. Here you find the decor and atmosphere of the 16th and 17th Centuries. The **Blossac Residence** (1730-1750) has a remarkable staircase (to the left as you go in). The timber-fronted houses (16th and 17th Centuries) run on into the **Rue de la Psalette** which follows the line of the massive early 19th-century

The Palace of the Parliament of Brittany before the 1994 fire.

The Town Hall.

chevet of the cathedral, and the **Rue Saint-Guillaume**. Beyond that is the busy Rue de la Monnaie.

A little further down the street to the left is the impressive and austere outline of **St. Peter's Cathedral** *(cathédrale Saint-Pierre)*. Building work started on the church in 1787 and was finally completed in 1844. It included certain features from an earlier church. Inside is a beautiful **reredos from Antwerp** (the life of the Virgin Mary and a Rod of Jesse, dating from the 16th Century).

Opposite the cathedral is the narrow **Rue des Portes-Mordelaises**. Nearby is a section of the mid 15th-century town walls.

If you go to the end of the street, you will come to the **Place des Lices**, where a large market is held every Saturday morning. There are several mid 17th-century mansions overlooking the square, all built in the local style using stone and timber. Note, too, **the covered markets** which are typical of the second half of the 19th Century.

At the bottom of the Lices is **St. Stephen's Church** *(église Saint-Etienne*, late 17th and early 18th Centuries), once the chapel of a convent. From St.Stephen's go down the Rue Nantaise to the **Duchesne Tower** (15th Century with later restoration) and the remains of the town walls. Our all too brief visit to Rennes is almost over. But, to recover from our fatigue, let us pause for a while in the **Thabor Gardens** to the North-East. Its 10 hectares were laid out in the grounds of the old Benedictine monastery of Saint-Melaine. The former abbey (now **Notre-Dame Church**) at the entrance to the gardens is

St. George's Palace.

open to the public. The transept crossing with its Norse arches and several 11th-century pillars in the nave (rare examples of Romanesque architecture in Brittany) have been incorporated into a 14th-century building. At the Eastern end of the Thabor Gardens stand the surprising buildings of **St. Vincent's High School**. It was built almost from start to finish in just eighteen months (1911-1912).

Anybody with an interest in rural life in and around the Rennes area would enjoy a visit to the **La Bintinais Folk Museum** *(écomusée de la Bintinais)* on the Châtillon road.

SAINT-BRIEUC (Côtes-d'Armor)

Standing on a hilltop, Côtes-d'Armor's biggest town is especially attractive because of its setting. Saint-Brieuc (alt. 325 ft.) has developed in a straggling sort of way between the steep-sided valleys of the R. Gouëdic to the East and the R. Gouët to the West. There are dozens of **bridges** in the town. The best place from which to admire the view is the Notre-Dame mound (to the North-West), the Alfred-de-Musset roundabout (to the North), **the Aubé Hill** (to the North-East) or the Huguin

Saint-Brieuc Cathedral.

Rennes: The Thabor Gardens.

roundabout (to the East behind the Renan High School). From here you can go to the Outdoor Theatre and to the Grandes Promenades Gardens by the Law Courts (1863).

In the Middle Ages, the town's bishop was Guillaume Pinchon. In the 13th Century, he defended it against the agents sent by Duke Pierre Mauclerc. He was beatified only thirteen years after his death. The main shopping street in Saint-Brieuc, the **Rue Saint-Guillaume**, was named after him.

Not far from this thoroughfare is **St. Stephen's Cathedral** (*cathédrale Saint-Etienne*, 1170-1248). It is an impressive building, as reminiscent of a fortress as of a cathedral and it was indeed used as a stronghold. The two towers date from the 14th Century. There are still some traces of the original building, e.g. certain parts of the main porch (13th Century), some of the capitals in the transept (13th Century) and St. Guillaume's tomb (mid 13th Century). Note the superb **Ascension Reredos** (1745).

In the streets round the cathedral are several corbelled houses, especially on the Place du Martray, and in the Rues Fardel, de Gouët and Houvenagle. Anybody interested in history will enjoy a visit to the museum (near the Champ-de-Mars).

SAINT-MALO (Ille-et-Vilaine)

Saint-Malo owes its exceptional wealth to its people whose passion for overcoming any obstacle in their way and whose spirit of independence led to their motto, *"Malouin first and foremost, Breton perhaps, French only if there's anything left"*. The Malouin character really does exist, created by centuries of battles on land and sea. The people still show a will to master their own destiny.

In the 17th Century, Saint-Malo was France's foremost harbour. It owed its prosperity to wide-ranging maritime trade based on cod-fishing off Newfoundland, which had been discovered by one of Saint-Malo's sons (Jacques Cartier), and the fur trade with Canada. Salt cod was sold in the countries bordering the Mediterranean. The ships then loaded their holds with alun from Rome which they delivered to the textile centres of Northern Europe. They also dealt in canvas and cotton with India and Spain. In the South Altantic, the Falkland Islands were visited by a local navigator named Gouin de Beauchesne in 1699; he named them "Iles Malouines" and they were colonised by adventurers from Saint-Malo from 1763 onwards. In the 18th Century, the locals were involved in the Slave Trade and they controlled the islands of Bourbon and France (now Réunion and Mauritius).

The difficult political and economic situation in which France found itself at the end of Louis XIV's reign forced

Saint-Malo.

Saint-Malo: The small keep.

Overleaf: A general view of Saint-Malo.

the Malouins to turn to a substitute form of trade that has been glorified in legends, i.e. privateering. Joint stock companies commissioned pirate ships in order to overcome the inadequacy of general trading. It was at this time that Sébastien Vauban and the architect Siméon Garangeau completed the building of the town's defences and the forts on the rocks that surrounded the bay (Fort Royal, Petit-Bé, Ile Herbois, Conchée, Cézembre, Ile Harbour etc.), all of them reefs that made the town impregnable.

During the French Revolution, Saint-Malo became known as Port-Malo. The harbour's commercial activities continued to decline. Surcouf was perhaps the most famous of the privateers but his exploits were isolated events. The golden age of the privateer was over. But Saint-Malo had not yet done with tragedy. A huge fire wiped out 80% of the town in August 1944. Today, though, Saint-Malo has been skilfully rebuilt in the monumental style of the town houses first erected in the 18th Century by Garangeau.

Enter the walled town by St. Vincent's Gate. The **castle**, now the town hall, dates from the 15th Century

except for the Eastern section, the Gallery, which was built in the 17th Century. The **Quiquengrogne Tower** backing onto the small keep was commissioned by Duchess Anne. The Great Keep, which was completed during the days of Duke Jean V and which was extended by the addition of the **massive tower** known as the "General" is now the local **museum**. Exhibits retrace the history of the privateers' town and its famous men.

A walk **round the ramparts** is quite magnificent, and it is the best way to see Saint-Malo. The walls (which were not destroyed by the great fire of August 1944) were designed by Siméon Garangeau, Vauban's pupil. It should, however, be pointed out that the North-Western section between the Bidouane Tower (17th Century) and the Queen's Fort (18th Century) was built last Century. Beyond the Bidouane Tower stands the statue of Robert Surcouf, pointing towards England. The Western section of the walls, which face seawards above Bon-Secours Beach, date from the Middle Ages; these are the smaller walls commissioned by Bishop Jean de Châtillon, stretching from the Bidouane Tower to the Holland Bastion. Beyond it is a statue of Jacques Cartier.

From the walls, the string of rocks surrounding the town is clearly visible - the **Petit-Bé** with its fort and the **Grand-Bé** where the writer François-René de Chateaubriand is buried. Further out to sea are **Cézembre** where the monks once lived, La Conchée Fort (1695), and **Fort-Harbour**, both of them designed by Sébastien Vauban.

A few of the houses escaped fire damage in 1944 e.g. the **Magon de la Lande** and **Asfeld Residences** near St. Louis' Gate. The granite shipowners' houses were designed by Garangeau in the 18th Century. The **La Gicquelais Residence** (Chateaubriand's birthplace) and the "glasshouse" (a wood and glass construction dating from the 16th Century) in the **Rue Pélicot** were also able to be saved. The buildings near the Dinan Gate to the West were rebuilt.

St. Vincent's Cathedral has now been fully restored and shows a combination of styles from various periods (12th to 20th Centuries). The West Front includes Renaissance, Classical and 18th-century archi-

A general view from the castle.

tecture. The 12th-century nave is roofed with great ogival arches in the style of the Anjou region, while the 13th-century **chancel** is typical of the Anglo-Norman style that is common in Brittany. The wonderful **great rose window** (1969-1972) was designed by Jean Le Moal and Bernard Allain, while the windows in the side aisles are by Max Ingrand.

SAINT-SERVAN

Saint-Servan used to be called Alet and the surrounding area was the Clos-Poulet. The large Gallo-Roman town became the capital of the Curiosolites and **Gallo-Roman sites** abound in the neighbourhood. One of them, at the foot of the Solidor Tower, dates from 390 A.D.

After being pillaged and set ablaze on several occasions during the Viking invasions, Alet was outranked in the 12th Century by Saint-Malo. The **Solidor Tower** was built in 1382 by Duke Jean IV of Brittany to keep control of the pirate town and prevent it from trading with Dinan. Solidor is a fine example of mediaeval military architecture. Today, it houses the **Cape Horners Museum**.

Bon-Secours Beach in Saint-Malo.

PARAMÉ

Now linked to Saint-Malo by the Sillon, or Causeway, Paramé is a large seaside resort. Take a stroll along the esplanade that follows the main beach and enjoy the picturesque scenery. When the tide is exceptionally high, the waves crash in across the road. The village of **Rothéneuf** has a **marine aquarium** and a few remains of Jacques Cartier's country house, the Portes-Cartier Farm.

It was on a **rocky headland** that dips down to the sea that Father Fouré (1839-1910) sculpted the legend of the Rothéneuf family. It took him 25 years to complete.

SAINT-POL-DE-LEON (Finistère)

The Rue Leclerc is the main thoroughfare in the town and it includes a number of old houses. The town has several interesting religious buildings, including St. Fiacre's Chapel (15th Century with 18th-century campanile) in the cemetery. There is also the 14th and 15th-century **Chapel of Our Lady of Le Kreizkêr** which has a remarkable spire designed to resemble the one on St. Peter's in Caen. It rises to a height of 254 ft.

Saint-Pol is also known for its **cathedral** built in the Norman style. It still has a few Romanesque features but most of the building is Gothic in style (13th - 16th Centuries). The light-coloured nave was built of Caen limestone. Around the chancel are small boxes bearing the names of the cathedral's canons and containing their skulls. The boxes are called the "shelves of night".

VANNES (Morbihan)

The town is built like an amphitheatre at the Northern end of an estuary flowing into the Golfe du Morbihan. Two narrow waterways join forces at the Southern end to form Vannes Harbour, which now has a wet dock.

Saint-Pol-de-Léon.

The old town walls in Vannes.

The surrounding hills reach no more than 71 ft. at their highest.

Start your visit of Vannes at the **Limur Mansion** to the North of the Rue Thiers; it is now the tourist office and Oyster Museum. From there, head for the Place Maurice-Marchais. Most of the urban activity of Vannes takes place on the four sides of this square. The **town hall** on the West side is a Neo-Renaissance building dating from 1886.

In the Rue Emile-Burgeault which runs into the square opposite the town hall, is the **governor's residence** (1655) standing at the end of a cul-de-sac. The street leads to the Place Henri IV lined with corbelled houses. In the Rue Saint-Salomon, a rabbit (at no.10) and imaginary animals (at no. 13) decorate the 16th-century house fronts. Next to the square is the Rue des Halles which has **more** half-timbered houses and the covered market built in a composite style (parts of it date from the 14th Century). Shopkeepers have been selling their wares here for many hundreds of years. Now, it houses the **Museum of Fine Arts**, the **Morbihan Gulf** and the **Sea** (*Musée des Beaux-Arts, du Golfe et de la Mer)*. The Roscanvec Residence (17th Century) houses the Natural Sciences Museum.

At the corner of the Rue Noë, **Vannes and his wife**, good ruddy-faced citizens that they are, look down on visitors. Flaubert saw them in 1846. In the same street is **Gaillard Castle**, an early 15th-century mansion house used by the Breton Parliament from 1456 to 1532. It is now an **archaeological museum**.

St. Peter's Cathedral *(cathédrale Saint-Pierre)* was largely rebuilt in the Flamboyant Gothic period and restored in the 19th Century. Of the original 13th-century building, all that remains is the North Tower on the front; a spire was added to it in the Romantic Period. The nave dates from 1450-1476, the chancel from 1774. Note also the organ (1742) and the treasure. In the chapter house (1782), there is a collection of old church plate. The most interesting item, though, is a 12th-century **marriage kist** decorated with paintings.

Leave by the Flamboyant Gothic North portal (1514) and take the Rue des Chanoines and the early 15th-century **Porte-Prison** down to St. Patern's Church (1727). In the streets nearby (Rue Saint-Gwenaël and Rue de la

The wash-houses in Vannes.

Bienfaisance), note the mediaeval houses, some of which are decorated. The Rue Fontaine and Rue Alain-le-Grand take you past the former Prefecture (County Hall, built in 1866) and on to the ramparts overlooking attractive gardens. The walls, topped by defensive battlements, incorporate parts of the 4th-century Roman wall. Two towers are still visible today i.e. the **Powder Tower** (16th Century) and the higher **Constable's Tower** (14th-15th Centuries).

As you go past the ramparts, you will see the splendid **wash-houses** (17th-18th Centuries) on the Rohan stream and the postern gate built in 1680. Beyond them is the harbour (St. Vincent's Gate dates from 1704; it lies to your right). There are a large number of old houses all along the basin. The **Place Gambetta** near the "Grand Canal" is one of the most delightful places in the town during the summer months.

Anybody interested in fish should be sure to visit the remarkable oceanic and tropical **aquarium** (on the Conleau road).

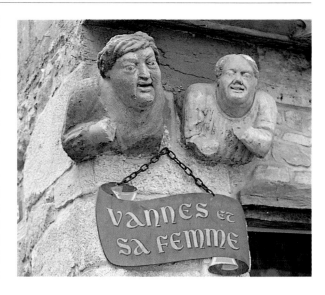

VITRÉ (Ille-et-Vilaine)

Vitré is one of the most charming towns in Brittany. Apart from its picturesque **streets** (Rue Baudrairie, Rue de la Poterie and Rue d'Embas), its old town walls are worth seeing. The superb **castle** (15th-16th Centuries) now houses a museum. The south wall of **Notre-Dame Church** (15th-16th Centuries) is a particularly fine piece of architecture. The railway station is built like a Neo-Gothic castle (1855).

Vitré Castle.

Breton Cuisine

Brittany is famous for its good food, and justifiably so. It has countless pancake houses and its restaurants serve menus in which seafood and fish have pride of place. Like all rural populations, the Bretons are very fond of pork-meat products (the region produces very high-quality chitterlings). The seafood platters are outstanding for the variety of shellfish they contain and fresh fish is served in a thousand and one different ways. For dessert, you can enjoy Breton specialities such as **kouign-amann**. And to wash it all down, there is a choice between cider, wine from Loire-Atlantique and butter milk which is usually drunk with pancakes.

Chitterlings.

A FEW BRETON SPECIALITIES...

Chitterlings: They are made from pork offal (stomach and large intestine). They are salted and left to mature for a week before being smoked over a wood fire (traditionally, wood from apple trees). The best-known chitterlings come from Lesneven (Finistère) and Guémené-sur-Scorff (Morbihan). They can be eaten hot or cold.

Cider: A drink obtained by the natural alcoholic fermentation of fresh apple juice. It is traditionally drunk in white cups with an orange-red rim called "bolées". A few farms still produce their own cider but most of it is factory-made. Reputably the best ciders come from Fouesnant (Finistère) and Pleudihen (Côtes d'Armor) where there is also a cider museum.

Scallops: A bivalve mollusc. The main centres of production are the roadstead off Brest and Saint-Brieuc Bay (Binic, Erquy, Saint-Quay-Portrieux). Some of the beds have been overfished and have now totally disappeared (Perros-Guirec). The scallop season lasts from October to March.

Cracklings: Dry pastries made from flour and eggs which crack or snap as you eat them (the French word "craquelin", which is known to have been in use for 700 years, is thought to be of Dutch origin). In the Middle Ages, they were also called "échaudés" because they were scalded in lightly-boiling water. Their shape has varied over the years and from region to region. In Brittany, cracklings are one of the specialities of the Dinan area where there are still a few, very rare, family busi-

Scallops.

Savoury pancakes.

Kouign-Amann.

nesses or larger factories, most notably in Les Champs-Géraux and Plumaudan (Côtes d'Armor).

Galettes: Savoury pancakes made from buckwheat flour, wheat flour (in some areas), eggs and salt. The batter is thick but is liquid enough to run off the ladle onto the **bilig** (a cast iron griddle) or into the frying pan. The pancakes must be cooked on both sides. They can be eaten as they are or filled with ham, mushrooms, chitterlings, eggs, cheese, tuna fish, smoked salmon etc. The recommended drink to accompany pancakes is cider or butter milk.

Kouign-amann: A cake. In Breton, **"kouign"** means "cake" and **"amann"** is the word for butter. First made c. 1865 in Douarnenez (Finistère) by a man named Scorolin, it is made from brioche dough and a large quantity of butter. Originally, it was baked in the baker's oven. It is served warm and is found all over Brittany but the real recipe is still the one used in Douarnenez.

Wine: Breton wines are now the speciality of the Loire-Atlantique where the vineyards cover an area of approximately 13,500 hectares, most of which (almost 10,000 hectares) produce Muscadet. Some 3,000 hectares produce Gros-Plant and a tiny area of 270 hectares produces Coteaux Ancenis. The recorded output in hectolitres is as follows: 660,000 of Muscadet, 246,000 of Gros-Plant, and 16,500 of Coteaux Ancenis, making a total of 922,500 hectolitres.

(Taken from the ***Dictionnaire de Bretagne*** by Michel Renouard, Nathalie Merrien and Joëlle Méar, pub. Editions Ouest-France,1992.

PHOTOGRAPHIC CREDITS

Patrick Béroul: pages 112, 113 (bottom), 117 (bottom).

Hervé Boulé: pages 10, 12, 18, 19, 22, 24, 25, 29, 31 (bottom), 34, 39, 40, 41(left), 42-43, 45 (bottom), 62-63, 65 (top, right), 65 (bottom), 66 (top), 67 (top), 69 (top), 70-71, 72 (top), 75 (middle), 76 (bottom), 78, 84, 88, 91, 96, 99, 100, 102, 103 (right), 104, 106, 107, 108 (right), 109, 113 (top), 114-115, 116, 117 (top), 119, 120.

Eric Cattin: pages 5, 56 (top), 60, 61, 64 (bottom), 69 (bottom), 98, 108 (left), 110 (bottom).

J-L. Cattin: page 92.

Hervé Champollion: pages 2 (bottom), 6 (top), 7 (bottom), 15, 20, 21, 23, 26, 31 (top), 36, 37, 38, 45 (top), 57, 58 (top), 59, 66 (bottom), 68, 72 (bottom), 90 (left), 93, 95, back cover.

CRTB: page 123 (bottom).

Marc Chauvin: Bertrand Demée: pages 64 (top), 73, 74, 75 (top, left), 75 (top, right).

Nicolas Fediaevsky: pages 13 (top), 14, 17, 97, 111 (top).

Claude Herlédan: pages 4, 7 (top), 11, 27, 28, 30, 32, 79, 80 (top), 121, 123, (bottom, left), 123 (bottom, right), 123 (top).

Imageo/Marc Chauvin: Front cover, pages 2 (top), 3, 8, 9, 13 (bottom), 44 (bottom), 46, 48, 49, 50, 55, 56 (bottom), 58 (bottom), 67 (bottom), 82, 85 (top), 101, 103 (left), 118 (bottom), 125.

Hervé Ledelis: pages 41 (right), 75 (bottom).

André Mauxion: page 65 (top, left).

Daniel Mingant: page 54.

Océanopolis: page 7 (middle) (2nd).

Michel Ogier: pages 16, 47, 51, 52, 110 (top).

Albert Pennec: pages 2 (middle), 7 (middle) (1st), 35, 45 (middle), 53, 76 (top), 80 (bottom), 81, 86, 87, 90 (right), 118 (top), 122 (top).

Franck Prével: pages 6 (middle), 6 (bottom), 33, 44 (top), 124.

Bruno Servel: pages 77, 83, 89, 94, 105, 111 (bottom).

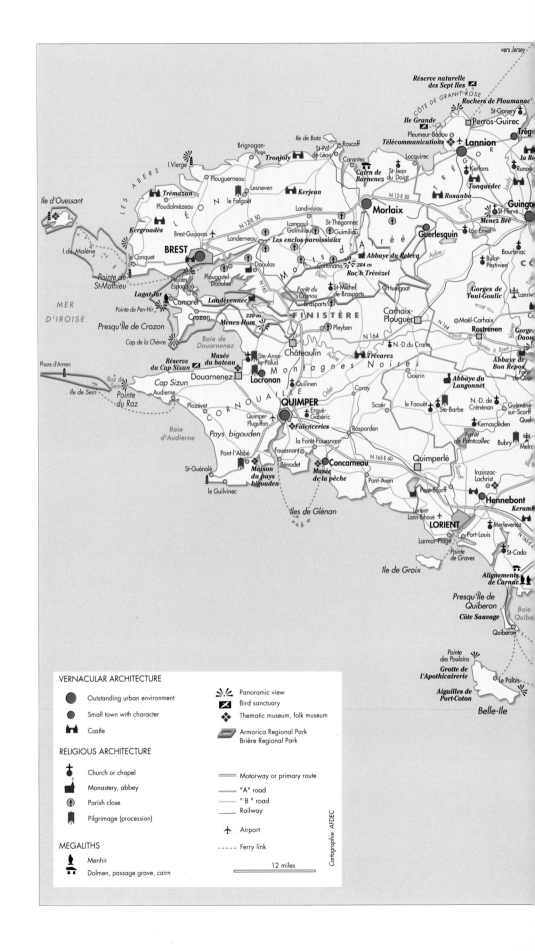

vers Jersey

Réserve naturelle
des Sept Iles

CÔTE DE GRANIT-ROSE
Rochers de Ploumanac'
St-Gonéry
Ile Grande
Pleumeur-Bodou   Perros-Guirec   Trég
Télécommunications   Lannion   la R
Locquirec   Kerfons   Runan
St-Pol-   Roscoff   Cairn de   St-Jean
de-Léon   Carantec   Barnenez   du Doigt   Tonquédec
Brignogan-   Rosanbo   Guingo
Plage   Tronjoly   St-Hervé
I. Vierge   Lesneven   N 12-E 50   Menez Bré
Plouguerneau   Kerjean   Morlaix   Loc Envel
Trémazan   le Falgoët   Landivisiau   St-Thégonnec   Guerlesquin
Ploudalmézeau   Lampaul-   Guimiliau   Bourbriac
Kergroadès   Brest-Guipavas   Guimiliau   Les enclos paroissiaux   Bulat-
le Conquet   Landerneau   Commana   384 m   Pestivien   Co
Ile d'Ouessant   Pte des   Daoulas   Roc'h Trévézel   Gorges de
Espagnols   Plougastel-   Forêt du   St-Michel   Toul-Goulic
I. de Molène   BREST   Daoulas   Cranou   de-Brasparts   Lanriv
Landévennec   Huelgoat
Pointe de   Lagat-Jar   Camaret   Brasparts   Gorge
St-Mathieu   Pointe de Pen-Hir   330 m   Carhaix-   Daou
Crozon   Menez Hom   FINISTÈRE   Plouguer   Rostrénen
MER   Cap de la Chèvre   Pleyben   N 164   Maël-Carhaix   Abbaye de
D'IROISE   Baie de   Châteaulin   N-D.du Crann   Bon Repos
Douarnenez   Ste-Anne-   Trévarez   Montagnes   Noires   Forêt
Phare d'Armen   Musée   la-Palud   Gourin   de Quér
du bateau   Quilinen   Abbaye du
Réserve   Locronan   Coray   Langonnet
du Cap Sizun   Douarnenez   Scaër   le Faouët   N-D. de
Raz de   Audierne   Odet   Crénénan   Guémené-
Sein   Cap Sizun   CORNOUAILLE   QUIMPER   Ste-Barbe   sur-Scorff
Ile de Sein   Plozévet   Quimper-   Ergué-   Rosporden   Quel
Pointe   Pluguffan   Gabéric   Forêt
du Raz   Pays bigouden   Faïenceries   de Pontcallec   Bubry
Baie   la Forêt-Fouesnant   Melr
d'Audierne   Pont-l'Abbé   Fouesnant   Quimperlé   Inzinzac-
St-Guénolé   Bénodet   Concarneau   Lochrist
Maison   Musée   Pont-Scorff   Hennebont
du pays   de la pêche   Pont-Aven   Keram
le Guilvinec   bigouden   Lorient-   Merlevenez
Lann-Bihoué   LORIENT   St-Cado
Iles de Glénan   Larmor-Plage   Port-Louis
Pointe
Ile de Groix   de Graves
Alignements
de Carnac

Presqu'île de
Quiberon
Côte Sauvage   Baie
Quibe

Quiberon

Pointe
des Poulains
Grotte de
l'Apothicairerie   Le Palais

Aiguilles de
Port-Coton

Belle-Ile

VERNACULAR ARCHITECTURE

- ● Outstanding urban environment
- ● Small town with character
- ⌂ Castle

RELIGIOUS ARCHITECTURE

- ✝ Church or chapel
- ♜ Monastery, abbey
- Parish close
- Pilgrimage (procession)

MEGALITHS

- Menhir
- Dolmen, passage grave, cairn

- Panoramic view
- Bird sanctuary
- Thematic museum, folk museum
- Armorica Regional Park
  Brière Regional Park

Motorway or primary route
"A" road
" B " road
Railway

✈ Airport
Ferry link

12 miles

Cartographie AFDEC

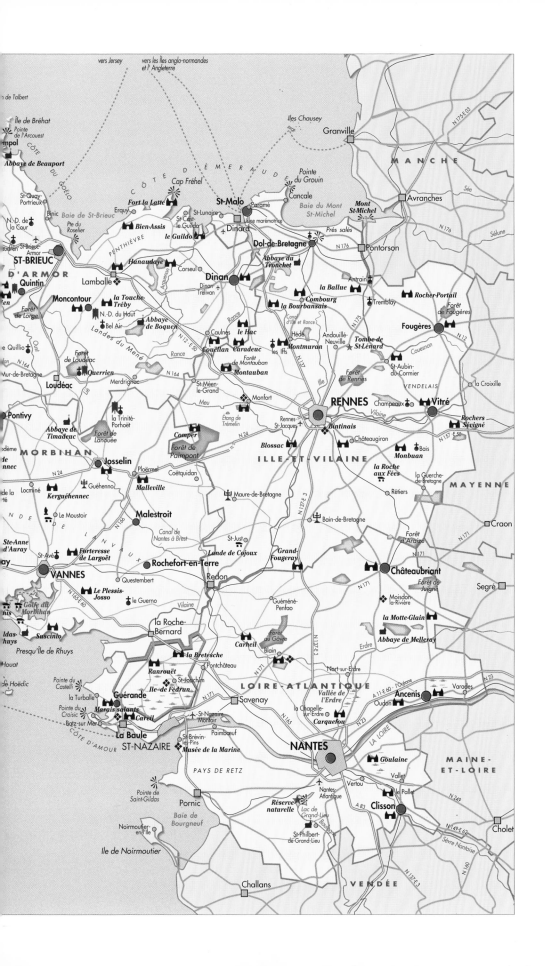

TABLE OF CONTENTS

Cet ouvrage a été imprimé par l'imprimerie Pollina, 85400 Luçon - n° 65139 - E
I.S.B.N. 2.7373.1203.5 - Dépôt légal : mai 1994
N° d'éditeur : 2525.01.06.05.94